The A-Zs of Worldbuilding

Building a Fictional World From Scratch

Rebekah Loper

Fantasia Hearth Press

Tulsa, Oklahoma

Copyright © 2017 by Rebekah Loper.

All rights reserved. No part of this publication may be reproduced or distributed in print or electronic form without prior permission of the author except in the case of brief quotations embodied in critical articles and reviews.

Permission is granted to copy only the exercise portions of this publication for personal use only. For further permissions (including academic permissions) or information, please contact: permissions@rebekahloper.com

Fantasia Hearth Press
PO Box 150321
Tulsa, OK 74115-0321

Loper, Rebekah – The A-Zs of Worldbuilding: Building a Fictional World From Scratch

First print edition: September 2017

Library of Congress Control Number: 2017914366

ISBN-13: 978-0692850558
ISBN-10: 0692850554
ISBN (e-book): 978-1537849386

Book cover image by: Footage Firm, Inc.

Dedication

To the A-Z Bloggers of 2014, who were the first eyes on what would become this book.

To the Ferrets, for their unending encouragement to never give up with my writing.

To Laura S., for helping me stay sane when life interferes with the creative process.

To Laura Weymouth, for being the first enthusiastic fan of The A-Zs of Worldbuilding (and all my writing, really).

To my husband, for putting up with my crankiness as I try to churn out words way too late in the evening.

To my mother, for teaching me to use my imagination.

And last, but not least, to my Creator, for equipping me with an imagination in the first place.

Table of Contents

Introduction 1

How to Use This Workbook 2

A is for Architecture 4

    'Architecture' Exercises 6

B is for Birth 12

    'Birth' Exercises 16

C is for Clothing 22

    'Clothing' Exercises 24

D is for Death 28

    'Death' Exercises 30

E is for Economy 36

    Economy' Exercises 38

F is for Food 46

    'Food' Exercises 48

G is for Geography 54

    'Geography' Exercises 57

H is for History 64

    'History' Exercises 66

I is for Interior Design 72

    'Interior Design' Exercises 74

J is for Judicial Systems 80

    'Judicial Systems' Exercises 81

K is for Knowledge 86

    'Knowledge' Exercises 88

L is for Language 96

    'Language' Exercises 98

M is for Military 106

    'Military' Exercises 107

N is for Nuptials 116
   'Nuptials' Exercises 120

O is for Oblectation 128
   'Oblectation' Exercises 131

P is for Plants 138
   'Plants' Exercises 141

Q is for Queens 150
   'Queens' Exercises 152

R is for Religion 158
   'Religion' Exercises 163

S is for Science 178
   'Science' Exercises 181

T is for Time 192
   'Time' Exercises 195

U is for Universe 200
   'Universe' Exercises 201

V is for Visual Arts 206
   'Visual Arts' Exercises 208

W is for Weapons & Warfare 212
   'Weapons & Warfare' Exercises 214

X is for Xenial 220
   'Xenial' Exercises 222

Y is for Youth 228
   'Youth' Exercises 231

Z is for Zoology 236
   'Zoology' Exercises 238

Congratulations! 243

Introduction

When I chose worldbuilding as my topic for the A-Z Blogging Challenge[1] in 2014, I knew I was taking on quite a task, and I had no idea what a resource it would turn into! This workbook is adapted from that series of blog posts. If you are interested in reading the original posts and comparing the two works, you can find those posts on my blog[2].

Worldbuilding applies to every story ever written. It is the set of rules you create which govern your world, whether it is historical fiction, contemporary fiction, or high fantasy. The only difference between all of those is the *types* of rules you create.

Your Authority as Author/Creator

Your story and your world are *yours*. You are creating it. You have the final say in what is acceptable in your world. You do not have to apologize for the way things are. You do, however, have to remain consistent with what you have established.

If you're writing speculative fiction, you don't get the option of not knowing your world. The hitch about creating fictional reality is that you have to make it all up. This can be incredibly freeing *or* frustrating, depending on your desires.

You must be prepared for the questions you will inevitably be asked. These will be questions about your world and your story; how and why you decided things. Hopefully many of these questions will come from an agent, editor, or publisher interested in your work. Pay attention to the questions they ask because readers will ask them as well. You are expected to know (or be able to extrapolate) the 'why' since it is your creation.

So What Is This All About?

If you're reading this book solely because you have an interest in worldbuilding and you're *not* writing a story, just ignore anything I say about plot, character development, and story conflict.

This workbook is geared toward speculative fiction writers who often don't have established land masses, let alone systems of government or family structures, when we begin. We literally create a world.

> ***Speculative fiction*** *is a catch-all term for genres like fantasy, science fiction, paranormal, and occasionally horror. Essentially, anything that can't (or, well, usually doesn't) happen in the world we live in belongs in the speculative fiction category.*

The worldbuilding exercises are designed to help you either build a world from scratch, or refine one you've already started on. Your knowledge doesn't have to be incredibly extensive, you just need enough to make your world realistic. The beauty of this workbook is that you can pick and choose which aspects you want to focus on.

If you are wanting to learn more about the writing process in general, *The A-Zs of Worldbuilding* will still be beneficial in helping you understand how setting and story interact.

---

[1] www.a-to-zchallenge.com
[2] rebekahloper.com/the-a-zs-of-worldbuilding

How to Use This Workbook

Each section of this workbook is, for the most part, self-contained. You do not have to work in any set order, and you can skip sections entirely if you feel they are not relevant to what you're creating. Take as much time as you need for each chapter, but try not to spend more than a few days on each one. You can also work on chapters simultaneously, if necessary. Just keep moving forward.

Establishing the Rules of Your Story

That said, particularly if you are worldbuilding for the setting of a story, I recommend you read through each chapter at least once, even if you don't think you'll be working with that topic in your story. You never know what you're going to need until you *need* it. Nothing is more frustrating than having to stop in the middle of a pivotal scene because you realized you don't know how something is supposed to work in your world.

Early on in a draft, it is easier to 'wing it' in those situations. But the further along in a story you get, the more rules you have already established for your readers, and you *must* stay consistent with those rules.

Increasing Momentum = Preventing Writer's Block

Another reason I suggest that you read through each chapter is because you never know what will spark your inspiration. The more ideas you have at your disposal, the less likely you are to get stuck further down the road.

Chase anything that catches your attention – even if it isn't for the story you'd planned to be working on. Don't lose your focus, but make sure to keep notes of anything that ignites your curiosity. You can't go back and work on it later if you've forgotten what it was.

What to Expect from Each Chapter

Each chapter will have two parts – a teaching section and an exercise section.

The teaching section will just be reading. There may be questions interspersed throughout the reading, but rest assured they are simply rhetorical at that stage. They are meant to make you ponder why things work the way they do in your world, but you won't need concrete answers to them. Yet.

The exercise section is where you will begin to apply what you've learned. The exercises immediately follow their respective chapters and consist of essay style questions. You don't have to answer all of them, and if you can't think of answers at that moment, don't worry about it. Remember, it's perfectly fine to bounce around the book.

Feel free to repeat the exercises[3] every time you create a new setting or culture, even within the same world. Every world has multiple facets of diversity, after all.

Are you ready? Let's build a world!

---

[3] Duplicate exercise sets are available for download on my website at rebekahloper.com/a-z-worldbuilding-downloads (password: 2017worldbuilding)

The A–Zs of Worldbuilding

A is for Architecture
Using Buildings to Enhance Your Setting

The first thing we're going to look at in *The A-Zs of Worldbuilding* is architecture.

I'm going to use a loose definition of architecture rather than a strict one. We'll look at all structures in general and not just the process of designing buildings. You can tell a lot about a group of people by looking at the buildings they construct. How they build is dependent on the terrain, resources, and climate where they live, and sometimes even their culture as well.

Terrain

What are the natural resources available?

The presence of trees means lumber can be processed, potentially into hand-hewn logs or sawn planks. Stone houses can be built from small boulders stacked together, or from quarried rock. Even soil can be used to build homes – sod and cob houses are wonderful examples of that in our world, though cob is much sturdier.

Cob is a building material made from a mixture of sand, dirt, straw, and water.
It is formed into walls by hand, and left to dry.
It is incredibly sturdy – there are cob houses in Europe that have survived for centuries.

What is the ground like?

Some of this will depend on the climate of the area. If the soil is too moist or too dry, it won't hold a foundation stable. Sometimes a foundation isn't necessary, especially if a structure is built directly onto bedrock. Anytime there is not a foundation, a structure is more likely to be destroyed, especially by wind or flood.

How can you use the geography to the builder's advantage?

Caves, as long as they are not too damp or slippery, or home to wild animals, can be an excellent substitute for actually building a house, particularly if your inhabitants have limited tools and supplies to build with. If an area tends to flood, hills are beneficial. Treehouses or building on stilts are an option if hills are unavailable.

Is there water nearby?

This is probably the most important question. No one is going to settle permanently where water can't be found. However, it doesn't have to be a river, creek, or lake. Some springs can be very small. There can also be water in underground aquifers, accessible through springs or dug wells. If there are healthy, vibrant trees around, there is definitely water nearby, even if it's not easily seen.

Climate

Is it hot or cold, wet or dry?

Certain accommodations need to be made depending on the fluctuation of temperatures in each season, and the type of weather typically seen.

Hot climates mean people need a way to stay cool. People will acclimate to the temperature but not beyond a certain point. They can build underground, when possible, or build so that plenty of air will circulate while still being shaded from direct sunlight.

Cold climates will require insulation. Losing heat can be deadly in certain temperatures. Windbreaks are also desirable, whether it is provided by trees or hills. Building underground can also help insulate a structure in cold climates, not just warm ones.

Wet climates will cause materials to deteriorate more quickly. Wood will need to be well-sealed and windows will need to be caulked somehow to prevent rain and moisture from coming in. Or, moisture will need to be allowed in and accommodations made in storing food away from the elements.

Dry climates are one of the easiest to work with. There won't be a problem with materials swelling and shrinking with exposure to moisture, and building quickly won't be as urgent. Dry climates also tend to be warmer ones, though the heat isn't as intense as humid heat is.

Culture

Are there any styles of homes reserved for certain members of society?

Think 'castles.' Anything that requires an extensive amount of materials and labor will be reserved for the wealthy, unless the building material is available in abundance.

Are there any shapes significant to the culture's history?

Is there any reason why a society would only construct square buildings, or even round ones? Climate can affect this, too. They may have found that round buildings hold up better in the wind.

Are there any shapes considered *sacred* to the culture's history?

What shapes are commonly used as religious icons, or placed in homes or at crossroads as talismans? Or are these types of shapes shunned, considered taboo, and only for use in temples or shrines, or only by royalty? Examples of shapes we would be familiar with are crosses, the Star of David, labyrinths, and crescent moons.

Other Inspiration

Look at the way other cultures live, especially ones that live in similar climates to the region you're creating. Find out why they built their homes the way they did. See how they integrate the natural resources available into their structures, and the adaptations they've made to deal with the climate.

Additionally, look at how they've built landmarks, especially palaces, temples, and cathedrals. Then look at how the common people live, and compare it to the extravagance. There will be similarities and differences. Use it for inspiration, working with the elements of your world to make something new. Just because you *can* build everything from scratch doesn't mean you *have* to.

'Architecture' Exercises

1. Take a moment to describe the immediate setting.

What is the climate and terrain like? How does the ground feel when you walk on it? What are the available resources for building structures? Where is the nearest source of water? What is it (river, lake, spring, etc.)?

___

2. What types of weather follow the different seasons?

Is the weather mild all year long, or are the season changes drastic, with very hot summers and extremely cold winters? If you've already made a map of your world, it will be helpful in figuring out the climate. Be mindful of the poles and equator. If your world is flat, you need to come up with the rules for how and why your weather works the way it does. Feel free to skip ahead to the Geography exercises (pg. 57) if you need to.

___

3. What types of structures are suitable for the resources on hand?

Bricks can be made from clay, stone homes can consist of natural rocks and boulders that are stacked together or chiseled to fit, and stone can also be quarried from rock deposits. Trees can be hewn by hand for log cabins, or cut into planks. In a place where there isn't stone or wood, or suitable earth for brickmaking, they may have to live in tents (made from animal hide or woven from hair), or make sod houses.

4. What types of shapes, both functional and sacred, are structured into a home?

Take careful consideration into how shapes are included. Round doors will require more care with hinges. A sacred shape may require some sort of reverence to go with it. Think of Jewish homes, with a mezuzah attached to the door frame. They will often kiss their fingers and press them to the mezuzah upon entering as an act of respect.

The A-Zs of Worldbuilding

5. Where is food prepared? Where is it stored?

Are there indoor kitchens? How is the residual heat managed? There might also be outdoor ovens and kitchens to be used in hot weather. Food storage, especially for long-term crop storage, must also be considered. Are there basements or root cellars (a basement can double as a root cellar, but root cellars are not always attached to a home)? Pantries or larders?

_____
_____
_____
_____
_____
_____
_____
_____
_____
_____

6. What about bathing and bathroom facilities?

Do people bathe in private, or public (like at a bathhouse), or do they have the option of either? What about using the toilet? Has indoor plumbing been invented, or is everyone using chamber pots that must be emptied? What about outhouses, completely separate from the home for hygiene's sake?

_____
_____
_____
_____
_____
_____
_____
_____
_____
_____

7. Briefly describe a typical upper-class home.

Upper-class can be anything from the wealthiest merchants, to the nobility, those viewed as heroes, and religious possibly religious figureheads, depending on the structure of your society. Which is seen as more prestigious – being wealthy enough to own a large estate, or being not needing enough land to be self-sufficient because they can buy everything? What sets an upper-class home apart from other homes?

_____

8. Briefly describe a typical lower-class home.

What do the everyday people live in? How cramped are their quarters, especially taking common family size into consideration? What few things are similar to an upper-class home, but lesser quality? Do commoners and peasants own the land their homes are on, or are they only tenants? How many people from a family typically live together and why?

_____

The A-Zs of Worldbuilding

9. What architecture resources are you using from our world for inspiration?

A is for Architecture

B is for Birth
The Wonder of Procreation

The birth of a child is a defining moment, and if you have a birth that takes place in your story, you can use it to add a richness and depth that you may not have realized before.

Birth has only become the recognized medical event (at least in first world countries) we know it as in the past couple of centuries. Before that, children were born at home. Sometimes a midwife attended, sometimes not. It all depended on if there was one available. Doctors were only called in if they were available and if something was definitely going *wrong*.

Invest in a good reference book for basic human anatomy and body function. It will come in handy for worldbuilding, especially when you need to deal with issues like birth, death, injuries, or disease. Even if your characters aren't strictly human.

A birth can mean an impending celebration, especially if the new child is the heir to anything, be it a notable inheritance, a seat of power, or a prophecy. A birth can also be mourned for all of those same reasons.

For simplicity, the term 'mother' will be used in this chapter and the corresponding exercises to refer to the being that is primarily responsible for the gestation of the offspring.

The Act of Birthing

Is birth viewed as a sacred event, something commonplace, or something taboo?

Is there any stigma around the act of giving birth? For some cultures, it is very sacred. It is the act of bringing a new life into the world. In other cultures, it's just another day. While the family may celebrate, there may not be any social events associated with it. In some cultures, especially extremely patriarchal ones, birthing may be taboo, considered to be 'women's business' only (there are exceptions to this); something necessary, but dirty, and to be over with as quickly as possible. Pregnancy and birth can be taboo even among matriarchal societies, especially if it's viewed as an event that incapacitates a valuable member of society.

Is birth a communal event, or a private one?

Who is present? The entire family may be required to witness the birth of the new child, or perhaps just the father. Maybe none of them are allowed in the room, and it's only the mother, the midwife, and possibly an attendant.

Or, perhaps for some reason, the mother is required to give birth alone.

There can be cultural and medical reasons for any of the above, and some of it will depend on the amount of knowledge your culture has about anatomy and reproduction.

Who is responsible for the medical well-being of the mother and child?

A midwife? A doctor? A robot? No, seriously, robot. Remember Star Wars? Or is it someone else (or some*thing* else) entirely? Just remember that the well-being of the mother and child starts long before birth – it starts at conception, at the least, and sometimes even before conception. Even if you don't depict the care that is received before that point, you need to know what it is because it will affect the health of both mother and child at the time of birth, and immediately following.

Which gender carries and gives birth to the child? How does gestation differ from human gestation, if applicable?

Even in our world, it's not always the female that carries the young. Think of seahorses – their reproduction is essentially the reverse of human reproduction. The female seahorse deposits her eggs with the male seahorse, and he fertilizes them and carries and gives birth to the young.

Then, of course, there are species that can change sex and fertilize their own eggs. Or they are both sexes at once. Your options are essentially limitless in this regard.

Post-Birth

Who cares for the child after birth?

Some of this may vary by the status the mother and/or father holds in society. It may not be considered appropriate for the woman to nurse her own infant. Some mothers won't care and will nurse their young anyway.

Sometimes it may vary by the child's gender. Perhaps in some societies, it is only appropriate for a mother to care for a daughter or son for so many days after birth before they are passed to the other spouse for rearing. There are a lot of potential complications that could arise from a situation like this, both emotionally and physically.

How are infants with perceived abnormalities dealt with?

Birthmarks

Birthmarks are often seen as something put there by a supernatural circumstance. They can be a kiss from a god/goddess, the sign of curse or a blessing, or just what we know them as – an abnormality in skin coloration. The perception of a birthmark (good/evil, normal/supernatural) can also change depending on the shape or location of the birthmark.

Deformities and Disabilities

Spina bifuda, cleft palates, misshapen or missing hands, feet, or limbs, brain development issues, etc., can all affect how a child is viewed by its parents. There are also *invisible* issues, and some of them may not be apparent until later in childhood. A child can be born with two perfect eyes but not be able to see. There's also the possibility of deafness, epilepsy, and conditions like Down syndrome and autism. This barely scratches the surface.

In some societies, it is impossible to provide the care needed for some of these conditions. If they aren't advanced enough to perform surgery, children with cleft palates will have a complicated life ahead of them, especially eating food.

Misshapen limbs, hands, or feet may make it impossible for a person to do manual labor later in life. In an agrarian society, they will be completely dependent on their family for survival.

Sadly, in less developed societies, children are often left to die from exposure when there is nothing that can be medically done for them. While it's terrible to think about, when you consider that your characters may not be able to take time away from ensuring their own survival or the survival of their other healthy children, it can be an acceptable motivation.

Societal Expectations

Is there a preferred gender?

If your society is patriarchal, matriarchal, or something else entirely, gender will change the perceived 'value' of a child at birth. At times, the blame for birthing a child of the 'wrong' gender may be placed on one of the parents, whether it is an accurate perception or not. Think of King Henry VIII, who practically bent over backwards to have a son, but it was his wives who shouldered the blame when they bore daughters. Of course, thanks to modern medicine, we now know it is the male's sperm which determines the sex of the child.

But that may not be the case in your world if reproduction occurs differently. Just keep in mind that no society is perfect. Even if gender doesn't play a role in the value of the child, there will likely be some part of their life where it *will* play a role.

Are any issues (gender, developmental problems, physical deformities, etc.) dealt with *in utero*?

This completely depends on how technologically advanced your fictional society is, or if they have magic that can tell the status of the unborn child. It will also depend on how much they are capable of doing *in utero*.

Detecting the sex of the child is one thing, and is fairly simple if they have an equivalent technique (whether magical or scientific) similar to our ultrasounds, or are capable of testing DNA. Detecting and correcting potential fetal health issues is another story.

If health issues are detectable, but not necessarily treatable, they may encourage a pregnancy to be terminated. Whether or not this is socially acceptable, or even *safe*, depends on the culture and amount of medical knowledge.

Are there any rituals associated with pregnancy and birth, or any stages in between? What significance do they hold?

In societies where there is a strong emphasis on tradition, or on the ability to create life, or anything where the new life is considered sacred in any manner, there are likely to be rituals and blessings associated with different stages of pregnancy.

However, any celebrations are likely to be held off until a point where the pregnancy is more likely to be viable. This may be different points of progression in different cultures. It may be after the first trimester, or the second, or when the mother is able to feel the child moving in the womb (also known as the quickening in some places). Celebrations may not be held at all until after the child has been born healthy, though, especially in a place where early pregnancy loss is frequent.

You will also need to decide if birthdates are something that needs to be noted, or if they simply go by seasons for remembering the age of a child. Additionally, there may be religious rituals for after the birth. These might involve anything from dedicating the child to the care of a specific deity, specific sacrifices that the parents must make on the behalf of the child, or receiving a certain mark (circumcision would be an example of this). Perhaps the infant must receive a blessing or prophecy by a local religious leader.

Other Inspiration

Take advantage of your research and talk to the women in your family. See if they know the stories of their births, their mothers' births, or their grandmothers'. Find out the story behind your birth, your parents, or siblings. Perhaps you'll even found out a funny (or sad) story about why someone ended up with the name they did! You never know what tidbits you'll find that will enrich the birth(s) in your story – whether it is rituals from another culture, a health struggle along the way, or the struggle to conceive at all.

The A-Zs of Worldbuilding

'Birth' Exercises

1. Is reproduction the same in your world as it is in ours?

Consider things like the act of conception, the length of the gestational period, and the actual birth itself. Is reproduction sexual (requiring genetic material from more than one parent) or asexual (a genetic clone, essentially)? Which gender carries and births offspring? Are there more than two sexes? Can only one sex gestate, or more than one? If the society is advanced enough, what scientific interferences are permissible?

_____
_____
_____
_____
_____
_____
_____
_____

2. Take a moment to consider the physical logistics of conception.

If your inhabitants are warm-blooded mammals, consider ovulation (when the egg is released for fertilization) and menstruation (what happens when the egg is not fertilized). While menstruation is a normal bodily function, the effect is still blood and sloughed tissue, and can still be a health risk. Cold-blooded creatures are more likely to lay eggs. Depending on the anatomy of the species you have created, how does conception work for each of them?

_____
_____
_____
_____
_____
_____
_____
_____

3. How is birth viewed in your world?

What expectations and stigma surround pregnancy? Is it sacred, commonplace, or taboo? What are some of the comments an expectant mother might hear from family, friends, or strangers? Is there a limit (imposed or implied) on the amount of children that can or should be born into a family?

4. What are some health risks to the mother and child which might occur during gestation and labor?

Some real-life, and very frightening, examples include pre-eclampsia, gestational diabetes, and hyperemesis gravidarum. That last one is basically really bad morning sickness that never goes away and it can lead to dehydration and malnutrition, which will affect mother and child. Pre-eclampsia is identified mainly by high blood pressure, and untreated it leads to seizures and death for the mother. If you are dealing with egg-laying creatures, there is the possibility of egg-binding, which is when the egg gets stuck in the reproductive tract.

The A-Zs of Worldbuilding

5. What about infertility?

Brainstorm some causes and treatments for infertility that might arise for your characters. Perhaps a species must go to a certain location in order to aid conception, or maybe improper hormone balances can decrease the chances of conception for humanoids. How much is known about the biological process of conception in your society? Do they know how it works, and which portions of DNA the parents contribute? What about the social stigma that might arise from not being able to have children? Is adoption available?

_____
_____
_____
_____
_____
_____
_____
_____

6. What happens at the actual birth?

What comforts and concessions are provided for the mother during labor and delivery, if any? Are fathers allowed any role, or is it just a midwife/healer/doctor and their assistants? Would the mother be required to give birth on her own, for any reason? What health complications might arise from that situation?

_____
_____
_____
_____
_____
_____
_____
_____

7. Who is responsible for the mother and child after birth?

What kind of aftercare is provided? Does it depend on how experienced the mother is? Are the mother and child given any bonding time, or is the child instantly whisked away for health evaluations? What cultural allowances are there? (IE: perhaps a female relative moves in to help care for the mother for the first several weeks after birth.)

8. What happens if the infant is not what was expected – either with gender, health, appearance, or anything else that your society might expect?

The leniency of these expectations may depend on who dictates the expectations. Of course, the personal disappointment of one or both of the parents is hard to overcome. But if a birthmark or deformity is deemed an omen or bad luck by the ruling authorities or religious figures, that can be impossible to overcome. A child may be abandoned if a medical condition is deemed incurable. Death by exposure is a common occurrence in cultures that abandon infants born with these types of issues.

The A-Zs of Worldbuilding

9. Are there any rituals associated with any stage of conception, gestation, and birth? It may be easier to answer this question if you have already played around with the Religion exercises (pg. 163).

These may be religious rites that have to be performed, or it can be as simple as the custom in many modern countries of throwing a baby shower. Also consider if a child is named at birth, or if the parents wait any amount of time to see if the child will survive before naming it. There may also be rituals, whether accurate or not, for determining gender.

_____

10. How does birth differ depending on social class, or location?

Not everyone's birth experience will be the same. Much of it will depend on what kind of access the mother has to experienced midwives or doctors. A couple out in the middle of nowhere may have to 'wing it' and hope there aren't any major complications. A peasant woman may have the same experience, regardless of her location. A wealthy mother will have access to almost anything she could want for during pregnancy. Unless, of course, she's stranded in the middle of nowhere, or has an overbearing spouse.

11. Take a moment and note down what resources you are using for birth in your story.

C is for Clothing
The Beauty & Function of Garb

We're all familiar with the *oh-so-elegant* clothes and ridiculously revealing armor (at least when it comes to women's armor) on the covers of fantasy books. There is very little realism in it. Some of this is because authors often have little say in their final covers, but when it is an accurate portrayal of what is *in* the book, it is often because writers may not know where to start in their research, so they emulate what they *are* familiar with, and of course there's just sex appeal which isn't bad by default, except when it means your character is dead in the first battle they fight.

Please take the time to research the type of garments your people would wear, and the textiles they have available. If you're doing a medieval fantasy (or something pseudo-feudal-European), I'll give you one hint: the lower class will not be wearing cotton. Especially peasants. The availability – and *affordability* – of cotton that we are spoiled with today has only happened in the past 200 years.

The only people in any world who dress impractically are either people who don't know better (which is especially enabled by our own technology-reliant lifestyle) or the rich. The rich determine *haute couture*, the high fashion which is expensive and luxurious. Think runway fashion.

It is the people who have to work – and work *hard* – to survive who are the ones that develop everyday, fashion. Their garments and accessories have to be functional, sturdy, reliable, and warm or cool as the weather calls for it.

Textiles

Fibers can come from multiple sources, whether local or distant. The further it must travel, though, the more expensive it will be.

They can be grown from plants. Some examples of plant fibers include linen (from the flax plant), hemp, and cotton.

They can come from animals – leather, wool, and silk are some familiar examples. Animal-produced fibers are infinitely more labor intensive to grow and harvest, but they can sometimes be more readily accessible because livestock can be simultaneously producing both meat and fiber at the same time.

The costs of all of these will fluctuate, depending on the resources available. During a drought, plant fiber prices will skyrocket, because they're going to be scarce.

During famine (which is almost always directly related to drought), the cost of animal fibers will skyrocket, as well as the price of meat. It could be especially damaging to someone who raises livestock specifically for fiber, because they may be forced to sell of much of their flock for meat, and lose their source of fiber by doing so.

However, any of these factors may change if it is a poor person bargaining with a wealthy person. Whoever has the money often has the advantage, because they are not lacking for food unless there is an overall food shortage.

Climate

The climate will directly influence the local fashions. All the fur in the world doesn't do a bit of good if your character is in a desert and will die of heat stroke with that much heavy clothing on. Likewise, cotton is not a sufficient safeguard from frostbite.

There's a reason the Inuit wear fur, and a reason why the Egyptians cultivated cotton. Each is appropriate for the environment and climate where they were located.

If your characters are in a climate where they will be dealing with a great deal of contact with water, leather is *not* a good textile option. Leather is, basically, cured skin. You know how when you've been in the tub for too long, your skin gets all wrinkly? Leather does the same thing, but because it's not a living structure anymore, it doesn't bounce back. Leather can be made waterproof, to an extent, but it has to be regularly maintained and if your characters are traveling a lot, they may not be able to keep up with it.

Also consider the terrain and vegetation in an area when designing the clothing of a region. If there is an abundance of thorns or sharp grasses, clothing will need to cover enough of the body – and be thick enough – to protect the skin from cuts and abrasions while still allowing for adequate airflow.

In climates with a lot of sunlight – whether cold or hot – with little shade, clothing will also have to become a barrier to prevent sunburn.

Function

We've already touched on part of the purpose of clothing, especially with the considerations for climate. After clothing has performed the basic function of protection from the elements, it starts to do more.

Clothing can be used to signify social status. It can be used to seduce. It can be used to disguise. The possibilities are endless, and much of it will be based on the culture of a society. Some of it will depend on technological advancements. How many of you have specifically dressed warmer than the outdoor temperature demanded simply because you knew you'd be spending hours in a chilled classroom? That wouldn't be possible without the invention of air conditioning.

What clothing looks like and what is considered acceptable will depend much on the religious culture, which types of textiles and garments are reserved for the upper classes, and whether or not a person has an assistant to help them dress.

Other Inspiration

Look at the ethnic dress of cultures that have similar climates to what you are developing. If possible, look at how dress has changed throughout history and with technological advancement. See if you can find correlations to the climate and available textiles. In history, different classes of people had vastly different fashions, too. Nobility and the working class had little in common when it came to clothes, so make allowances in your worldbuilding for that.

The A-Zs of Worldbuilding

'Clothing' Exercises

1. What textiles are readily available through trade or craft?

Fibers come from multiple sources, whether local or distant. Plant fibers can include things like cotton, hemp, or linen (which is made from flax). Animal textiles can include various kinds of wool, silk, leather, and even feathers. Make note if a textile is woven (does not stretch) or knit (can stretch if constructed with the appropriate method). Leather is made of animal skin, and so it must go through a curing process to be preserved.

_____
_____
_____
_____
_____
_____
_____
_____

2. What is the most commonly available textile?

This would be something that even the poorest would wear because it's so readily available and easily made. What is the source of the fibers used to construct it?

_____
_____
_____
_____
_____
_____
_____
_____

3. What's the most expensive textile?
Is this limited to certain people, either by social status and/or financial status? What is it made of? How hard is it to come by? Where does it originate?

4. What elements do your characters need to protect themselves from in their natural environment?
What is the climate like? Are there any temperature extremes to account for? What types of fluctuations are there between the seasons? Do they need to protect themselves from the terrain at all?

5. Think about body image. How does fashion evolve from that?
What is accentuated, and what is hidden? What is fetishized, or taboo? Why? How does it affect garment styles? Do different genders dress differently?

_____
_____
_____
_____
_____
_____
_____
_____
_____

6. Describe a day-to-day garment for lower-class, middle-class, and upper-class characters.
Give yourself something to draw inspiration from for the rest of your garments and fashion in your world. If you'd rather draw examples than describe them, do that! You may want to look up croquis *(fashion figure templates) online so you have a template to work from. How are different colors used within a society, either by gender, social class, or for occasions such as weddings or mourning?*

_____
_____
_____
_____
_____
_____
_____
_____
_____

7. What resources are you using for the fashions in your world?

D is for Death
Don't Fear the Reaper

Death is as much a part of life as birth, and in speculative fiction it can be a very important aspect of plot and character development. How a character deals with death is going to be affected by what they believe about the afterlife and what their culture believes. However, personal beliefs can often override cultural beliefs. If you have skipped ahead to the Religion[4] section, or if you already have some notes jotted somewhere about religion in your world, you might want to reference them as you work through this section.

Preparing the Body

Decomposition begins immediately when someone dies. There are several factors that will determine *how* the corpse is dealt with.

First off, how did they die? How much medical knowledge exists, especially about the transmission of disease? Anyone who dies from something contagious must have their remains dealt with quickly to avoid the spread of the disease to others – though sometimes it spreads too fast to make much difference.

Even if the deceased was relatively healthy, the decomposition of flesh is not going to be pleasant nor sanitary to be around for very long. The general rule of thumb is that the warmer and more humid the environment is, the faster decomposition will set in. There are exceptions: extremely hot and dry weather cause a mummification effect if everything is just right. Other factors will be the climate and the terrain – and yes, the climate and terrain really do have *so much* to do with almost every aspect of life. These will be recurring factors throughout this entire workbook.

The most common methods of dealing with a corpse in our world are burial (in the ground), cremation (burning the body – be aware that it takes an extremely hot fire to turn bone to ash), entombment (such as the cairns, though mausoleums are another option), mummification (preserving the body, often for transport and later entombment, sometimes for public display), and sky burial (leaving the body exposed to wild animals and the elements until the skeleton has been cleaned of tissue).

Cairns are, quite simply, stacks of rocks and stones. They can be very small or very large, and have multiple purposes – everything from landmarks to graves.

Burial is not an easy way to deal with dead bodies, especially since they need to be buried deeply to prevent the body being uncovered by weather or wild animals, or even grave robbers. If there is no heavy machinery, it must all be done by manual power, and sometimes the terrain just doesn't cooperate. If the ground is too rocky, or if it's frozen, burial may be impossible. Some options in lieu of burial are a shallow grave covered by a cairn, cremation, or mummification (which can be more work than burial itself). Or even cannibalism, if you want your story to be truly gruesome.

---

[4] *R is for Religion*, pg. 158

However, even in the best climates, unexpected weather can always interfere, so there needs to be a plan for how a body is dealt with in inclement weather. When the climate is known to have extremes (very hot summers and/or very cold winters) a culture will have protocol in place for dealing with corpses during inclement weather. In a place with extremely harsh winters, the inhabitants may have a communal cave where they place the dead to await spring burial. Or they may just use the cave for entombment year-round.

Bidding Farewell

One aspect of death that many modern societies have lost is caring for the deceased and preparing them for burial (note: *burial* will be used by default to represent all manners of disposition of the body from this point on), though there are some cultural exceptions to this.

It is more common these days for bodies to be taken away and prepared by paid morticians, and then to be buried according to what the law dictates – though those laws are in place for public health.

If there are no morticians, cemeteries, or crematoriums, though, what happens?

Perhaps the family members care for the body, in whatever way their culture dictates. They may wash it and dress the corpse in finery. Perhaps runes or talismans must be properly place on the body, or some ritual performed, to ensure the soul enters the afterlife. Or maybe it is simply to comfort the bereaved.

Into the Afterlife

This will likely play heavily into the religion(s) you've created for your world. Is there a belief in the afterlife, or not? Those who have the authority to speak on the afterlife in your world may have significant reasons to take advantage of those beliefs, perhaps even finding a way to make a profit off of them. You, as the world-builder, have the authority to decide which beliefs are true or not in your world, but differing opinions about the afterlife can shape culture and even provide the source for many conflicts.

Whether the afterlife consists of reward, punishment, or nothingness, there are certain to be people interested in changing what their afterlife may consist of. How that manifests – be it a quest for immortality or through recklessness – can be fantastic story fodder.

Other Inspiration

If you've started to toy with religions for your world and characters already, look through cultural history and mythology and see what you can find that has a similar belief system, and how they might deal with death and questions about the afterlife. Don't copy things exactly, and certainly don't call them your own, but study them to see how the beliefs and cultural nuances work together so you can get an idea of how to make it work better in your story.

If you haven't played around with religion yet, don't worry. Look at the story idea you're working on. Death is often an integral part of plot, so look at why it's happening in your story and how it's supposed to affect your characters. Start fashioning things from there, and how you need it to work with your story.

'Death' Exercises

1. How much medical knowledge exists?

Do people know how to dispose of dead bodies to prevent the spread of disease?

2. How are the bodies disposed of?

Are the deceased buried, or does the climate or terrain inhibit that? What are the customs that have developed to accommodate those situations?

D is for Death

3. What if the weather is the complete opposite of what your characters are used to, and someone has died?
How do they deal with the situation? If, say, cremation is taboo to them, but it is the only option available (let's say the ground is frozen), how is that situation dealt with?

4. Who prepares the body for disposal?
Is this something considered to be an honor, or is it a responsibility people avoid? Are there any superstitions about dead bodies that may affect people's behavior about this? How might children misinterpret these types of situations?

The A-Zs of Worldbuilding

5. What happens at a typical funeral?

Is it a simple commemoration of the dead, or an elaborate ceremony? What parts of the funeral have been included, traditionally, for so long that no one remembers why they are? What is something someone would never do at a funeral?

_____

_____

_____

_____

_____

_____

_____

_____

_____

6. Is death seen as *the* end, or is it the next stage in life?

Why do your characters believe what they do about the afterlife? What do you, as the creator of your world, say is true about the afterlife?

_____

_____

_____

_____

_____

_____

_____

_____

7. If there is an afterlife, are there any criteria that must be met for certain outcomes?

Should your character have lived a certain way, performed certain deeds, perhaps paid the right priests? Are there any rituals that have to be performed, either while the deceased was alive or dead, to aid their passage? Are the deceased required to take supplies with them into the afterlife (such as food or weapons)?

_____
_____
_____
_____
_____
_____
_____
_____

8. If the outcome of the afterlife depends on any rituals for the deceased, what happens if something goes wrong?

A ritual-dependent afterlife is something that will have both a huge cultural impact and a will be rich for storytelling. If it is required for someone to have mourning prayers spoken by a family member, but they are estranged or orphaned, then they may be going through life trying to find a substitute family, even subconsciously, for example. But what if someone can also be condemned in the afterlife by the actions of the living? Ideas are everywhere!

_____
_____
_____
_____
_____
_____
_____
_____

The A-Zs of Worldbuilding

9. What resources are you using for death and funeral customs in your world?

D is for Death

E is for Economy
Establishing Production, Trade, and Money in Fictional Worlds

I'll be honest here: economics is not my expertise. But here's what is so beautiful about economics in speculative fiction: it can be as simple or as complicated as you like.

That said, you can't get away with *no* economics. Somewhere along the line, your characters are either going to need to acquire things or get rid of things. Unless they're foraging in the wilderness (which is not as simple as it sounds) or just throwing stuff out, they will need to buy, sell, or trade goods.

Production

The goods that people can produce are the bedrock of an economy. By looking at the resources available to your characters, you'll see what they can produce.

If there is arable land, agriculture will quickly become one of the main sources of production. There are many other natural resources, as well. Minerals, metals, lumber, and even water are also examples of non-manmade goods that will be in high demand.

The level of production, and import and export, will be dependent on how self-sufficient people are in different cultures. Anything that can be quickly produced in abundance will be a good export option as long as there is someone who needs it elsewhere. Anything that can't be made or grown easily will be imported from other places.

Don't forget the value of skills. Not everyone can do everything, and when you need a wall replaced or a house built, you're going to be willing to give up valuable assets for someone who knows how to do it right.

There may also be legal limits established by a government (whether just or not) that inhabitants must work with. Hunting may be forbidden in the king's forest, for example. It doesn't matter if your family is starving and lives right next to that forest. One may need to purchase licenses and rights to produce certain items or harvest certain natural resources, as well.

Trade

There are many ways trade can be accomplished between interested parties. It can be a barter, where another product is directly traded for the desired product. Skills can even be used for barter – a mending job in exchange for a loaf of bread, for example.

One aspect of the barter system, though, is that there can be one party who places an exorbitant value on an item, even if that item is not worth much monetarily. They may simply be unwilling to give something up, or the sentimental value far outweighs any want or need.

More commonly familiar to those of us in first world countries is the trade of currency – we exchange money for goods. That also brings inflation into play, especially if the actual currency does not consist of anything that is valuable, such as paper money. If there isn't actual collateral for every bit of paper money in circulation, it makes the money worth less, and eventually that means you have to 'pay more' for goods.

Regulation

Where there is active trade and a governing body, there is always sure to be taxes.

If there is currency, other than weighted precious metals and gems (or whatever is deemed most valuable within a culture) there will be banks.

In all likelihood, someone will decide that trade needs to be regulated, taxes levied, and monies kept 'honest.' No matter what, someone somewhere will try to counterfeit the standard form of payment. Whether that is silver coins dipped in gold to appear more valuable, or even a sack of beans made heavier by mixing rocks in.

Currency

Currency can be *fun*.

Currency can be *anything*.

Usually, it consists of something that is not too terribly hard to come by, but is also worth quite a bit to a culture.

A look through our world's history will show that currency has consisted of everything from cacao beans to bricks of dried tea leaves. Of course, many of us are most familiar with paper currency, metal coins, and 'virtual' money like credit cards.

Less technologically advanced societies will likely use sustainable forms of currency, like the cacao beans and tea leaves mentioned above. If your world has some sort of internet-type technology, virtual money may change hands as well. Your sky is limitless.

Other Inspiration

Don't forget that you can make economics simple or complicated for your story – it's completely your decision. Don't make your brain melt. Just get the story written. At the very least, know the basics of your money system, and what goods are available in which regions.

If economics play a large role in your story, you will have to be spend more time in this area. Economics and politics often go hand in hand, so be sure to look at points in our history that may give you insight into how the two mesh, and how they don't mesh well at all. It can be a great source of conflict in your plot.

Also consider how economics can be disrupted by some sort of catastrophe – natural disasters, such as famine or floods, can drastically impact the availability and production of goods, especially agriculture and food. Wars can cut off access to imported or exported goods that were previously considered dependable. Taxes may be increased to pay for war expenses, and rationing may be put in place to prevent a resource from vanishing completely.

Ultimately, economics is about your inhabitants acquiring what they want and need, and bargaining with others who have what they want or need, no matter whether that is a trade of skills and products, or currency and products.

'Economy' Exercises

1. Who, if anyone, owns the majority of land available?

Does the concept of private property exist? If so, who is permitted to own property – the everyday people, or is land ownership only for those with titles or wealth, or does the ruling monarch own all the land by default? When those situations are the case, is there any obligation the ruling authorities have to provide for their subjects, and to let them work the land?

2. How self-sufficient are people? How many natural resources are available at no cost?

The more self-sufficient people are, the less they rely on trade for either their livelihood, or for their necessities. Money often has little value to people who know how to live off the land and make almost everything they need. Trade and economy will often develop out of what people lack, or what they desire for enjoyment.

3. What products and resources are available in abundance? What is rare, or takes more effort to produce?
People are more likely to part with something that is easily replaceable, and usually for less money as well. Things that are rare or have a high sentimental value will be costly to the buyer.

4. Who is in charge of the acquisition and/or production of rare goods?
This could be a closely guarded family secret, or something that a community works on together. It will depend on the manpower required to produce it.

5. Is a bartering or monetary system in place? What about a combination of both?

Look at the society – do they place more value on survival, or the accumulation of wealth? Bartering is a better system for those who are needing things to tide them over while they wait on funds, or if they are able to produce goods to trade. Monetary systems usually work best in societies that place a social status on wealth. There are exceptions, but those are good starting places.

6. Who (if anyone) controls the flow of commerce and money within a region?

Is it on the local level, or a national one? Options would include merchant guilds, a chamber of commerce, and even local government officials like mayors or tax collectors. On national levels, it could be representatives of the ruling figures.

7. Are there banks? Are they regulated by the government?

Banks can serve many functions within a community. They may be able to exchange foreign currencies for local ones, which will be particularly handy for traveling merchants. They may have some responsibility for watching for forged currencies. They can also offer security for people transporting large portions of money from one place to another – a network of banks might allow account holders to access from any bank, whether the funds are physically held there or not. A royal or official treasury may also serve many of these functions.

8. Is there a specific type of currency endorsed and regulated by the government? Describe it.

Government may step in to regulate currency to help minimize forgery, help control inflation, and prevent economic collapse. For science fiction and futuristic societies, don't forget that currency might be digital!

The A-Zs of Worldbuilding

9. Can people smelt their own precious metals for coinage, or use raw weight for whatever they desire to purchase?

Gold dust can be weighed out into whatever amount a merchant desires, and coins can also be weighed to make sure they are 'true.' There are ways to work around this.

10. What are the main import and export items? How are they transported?

When considering import and export items, make sure to keep in mind that some things may be perishable. If something has either a long shelf life, or is a non-perishable good, it can travel far to be sold. However, if it will only last a few days to a few weeks, it either has to be transported quickly, or it can't travel far. Societies that are more technologically or magically advanced may be able to help with modes of preservation, though.

11. Are there special taxes (tariffs) levied on trade items, whether it is staying local, or if it has been imported or exported? Who is in charge of regulating and collecting those taxes?

Imported and exported items could have additional taxes, too, and they could even have multiple taxes when they are sold or acquired to merchants, and then to the consumer. There may also be a sales tax.

___

12. Is personal or business income tracked, and are additional taxes taken from it?

Depending on how the government is run, these taxes can be reasonable or downright monstrous, so look at the motivations for collecting such taxes as well.

The A-Zs of Worldbuilding

13. What economic resources are you using for your worldbuilding?

E is for Economy

F is for Food
Sustenance for Body & Soul

Food is an integral part of every society, because everyone needs to eat to survive. It doesn't matter if they are vampires who only drink blood or aliens who absorb what they need through their skin – they are still consuming and absorbing the nutrients necessary to their survival.

The Function of Food

Obviously, life is dependent on being able to consume the necessary nutrients to keep the physical form functioning. Food does not have to taste good or look pleasant to accomplish this, but if food *is* delicious and visually appealing it increases the chances that someone will *want* to eat it.

How food is acquired and prepared will affect both how it tastes and appears to different individuals. There is a different appreciation for food that has been grown, harvested and prepared from the garden, or hunted and foraged from the wild by someone individually. Societal apathy can set in when food is available in abundance from places like supermarkets, where it's now possible for people to go an entire lifetime without knowing that meat must be harvested from living creatures.

When it comes to meat, the difference is huge. When an animal has been raised from birth (or close to it), then humanely slaughtered, it not only tastes different but is better appreciated by those who consume it. When the consumer is separated from that process entirely, only being exposed to the finished product, there is a disconnection about what food actually is and its worth.

However, it's not a reasonable expectation for each individual member of society to produce *all* of their own food. While historical societies did not have grocery stores and supermarkets like we're familiar with today, there were markets where farmers and vendors would bring their surplus goods – food and otherwise – for others to acquire. Supermarkets and grocery stores are just those original markets on steroids, with the purchase protocols streamlined for modern consumers.

In an agrarian society, the difference between abundance and starvation can be a matter of timing. If the grains don't get planted or the spring garden put in, or if the livestock don't breed or birth their young successfully, there won't be enough food.

Flood, fire, drought, extended winters, or long rainy seasons can all affect the production of food and cause famine.

In extreme climates, like an arctic tundra or desert, look at *why* inhabitants eat what they eat. If there is a short growing season, or only a small amount of water for irrigation, food cultivation becomes limited to what is necessary for survival. In colder climates, people will need to consume more protein and fat to stay warm. In hot environments, the consumption of salt is very important because it is lost through sweat, and without salt the body cannot absorb water.

The Meaning of Food

Food is often an important part of many cultural feasts or holidays. The preparation of certain dishes can be very ritualistic, and foods can have significant meaning for seasons of life, they can have spiritual connotations, and they can have societal and cultural implications.

One well-known religious example would be the representation of leaven and sin in Judeo-Christian teaching. Additionally, if a religion practices animal sacrifice, there is almost always some consumption of that sacrifice as well, whether by the priests, the family that provided the offering, or the community as a whole.

Societal implications can be as simple as how salads and smoothies (or quiche, in my husband's case) can be 'girly' foods unfit for masculine consumption. There's also the flipside – steak and potatoes is considered 'man food' in many places. Even though that doesn't stop women from eating steak or potatoes, *men* consider it superior to other options. Like salad.

Food can take on personal meaning, as well. It's not difficult for a person to pick out a dish that embodies their childhood, or recall a meal that will never be the same again, even if it was a longtime a favorite, if bad news was received while that dish was being prepared or consumed.

Recipes can also be lost over the course of time. Someone may have thought it was recorded somewhere, only to find that it never was long after the death of whoever prepared the family dish. Ingredients may become scarce or extinct, or just not available because someone moves away from a region.

Other Inspiration

Look at traditional foods from different cultures, see what you can draw inspiration from. Holiday dishes can be extremely varied from place to place, even for the *same* holidays.

Religious feasts can have a huge amount of symbolism in them – take a look at a Passover Seder plate, for example. Each item (all food) on the plate have a very significant meaning attached to them.

Don't forget to consider foods that might be forbidden or taboo as well, either because of social status, environmental concerns, or animal cruelty. Traditional foods might have very high expectations, as well – with no wiggle-room for innovation or reinterpretation.

Once you get sucked into the diversity of food and the different meanings it can have, you'll have a whole new world open up in your stories, and possibly in your kitchen, too.

'Food' Exercises

1. What types of food, spices, and herbs are grown and produced locally?

What livestock and plants are native to a region? These will be the first that are used for sustenance, especially when a place is being newly settled.

2. What types of food, spices, and herbs have to be obtained from non-local sources?

How far do they have to travel? If the goods are perishable, how do they transport them without spoilage?

3. What do the livestock eat?

Does it affect how their meat, eggs, or milk tastes? Is one type preferred over another, such as pasture-raised, or grain-fed?

4. Briefly describe the daily sustenance for a people from the peasant, middle, and royal classes.

Peasant and middle class will eat mostly local fare. Middle class may, occasionally, sample some more luxurious items, but not very often. Royalty will also eat a lot of local food, but will be able to indulge in foreign fare more often. Peasants will have the least access to a variety of foods, despite being responsible for growing them, depending on the society you've set up.

The A-Zs of Worldbuilding

5. What would be the standard fare at a local pub, tavern, or inn?

You'll need to think about the size of staff working in the kitchen at one of these places. Fare is likely to be things that can be made in great quantity by a few people. Very little of it will be made 'to order,' if anything.

_____
_____
_____
_____
_____
_____
_____
_____

6. What dishes have become culturally iconic?

What dishes and spices is the region and/or country known for? This will branch off from unique, local resources – certain flavor combinations, the ingredients available, etc. In immigrant cultures, though, it may also be an adaptation, a way to recreate a beloved cultural dish as closely as possible without the original ingredients. Sometimes the substitutes may become more popular.

_____
_____
_____
_____
_____
_____
_____
_____

7. Are there any holidays that have traditional foods associated with them? What about a fast? How might the fast be broken?

This can be as broad as the idea of Christmas cookies, or more specific, like the roasted lamb that was served at Passover in ancient times, with a very particular way it had to be slaughtered and roasted.

8. Are there any foods that, no matter when they are consumed, have a particular significance to them?

A prime example would be Holy Communion. There isn't a set time for partaking of Communion within the church, but there are times when it is nearly certain that it will be taken. But it can be done at any time. And the elements are universally recognized – bread and wine as the body and blood of Christ.

The A-Zs of Worldbuilding

9. What foods are forbidden?

Certain types of food may be limited or forbidden. There could be health or religious reasons. Even cultural reasons – perhaps a type of food is a beloved icon of a neighbor they are at war with, or something that is only eaten by one gender.

_____
_____
_____
_____
_____
_____
_____

10. What foods are available when?

Some items will only be available during certain growing seasons. Berries, for example, are most abundant during the spring and early summer. Apples are ready for harvest in the late summer or fall, depending on the variety. Because most plant life goes dormant during the winter, food must be preserved if it is to last out of season. Salt, sugar, fermentation (different bacteria strains in different regions will affect taste), dehydration, etc., are all ways of preserving food for storage. What types of dishes have been developed from this?

_____
_____
_____
_____
_____
_____
_____

11. What resources are you using for creating food in your world?

G is for Geography
Know Where Your Story Is – Literally

Figuring out the geography of your world is important to do *early* in your story, otherwise you may end up with things spread out way too far for what you've intended, or maybe even a desert oasis in the middle of the arctic tundra. Modeling your world after Earth makes figuring out climates infinitely easier, as you have a working model. But if you veer from that either accidentally or purposely, don't worry. Artistic license is a beautiful thing.

The beauty of fantasy writing is that you can get away with making up a lot of stuff. Science fiction will be a stricter, depending on your intended audience.

The Lay of the Land

One of my favorite ways to discover the geography of my fictional worlds is to 'talk' to my characters. I find out where they are from, what common landmarks are in their area, what the scenery looks like.

Focus on the physical aspects of the land, things that cannot be easily altered. Mountains, creeks, rivers, forests, etc. *Not* buildings – unless something has been carved into a mountainside – or towns, or cities.

Look at the terrain, whether there are fields and plains or a lot of hills and trees. The quality of the soil will help determine where people settle, because rich, fertile soil is where they will be able to grow food. Good topsoil with rich vegetation is also less likely to be swept away in floodwater, because it is capable of absorbing more water while the vegetation holds it in place. Everything has a saturation limit, though. Drought and compacted earth make flooding more likely during heavy rainfall, no matter the soil quality.

If the area is prone to flooding, earthquakes, or volcanoes, the terrain may change frequently and rapidly. It will also affect how much settling is actually possible in that location, unless there are ways of controlling those natural forces. And, well, in fantasy and science fiction... you can work wonders!

Terrain and climate go hand in hand, though, so you need to keep a few more things in mind as you worldbuild at this stage.

Real-life research is very valuable here, unless the laws of nature work on a completely different system for your story.

However, unless you have a story-specific reason for changing things up, or you have an obsession with science and the know-how to make it work, I highly recommend modeling your world after the appropriate Earth climate for your character's habitation, unless you're writing alien planets for science fiction. It will be easier for your readers to relate to, and it also saves you a lot of headaches.

There can be a lot of variables even within climate and terrain, though. For example, a desert doesn't have to be hot, and even hot deserts are cold at night because there's nothing to hold the heat in (vegetation has insulating properties) once the sun has set.

If you're writing fantasy, you can have some exceptions. It is certainly possible to have a hot desert right next door to the arctic tundra if, say, the climate is controlled by magic, deities, or technology. But keep in mind that you can only ask your readers to suspend their 'belief' to a certain extent, so save it for the important things.

Making a Map

Maps are an invaluable source for fantasy and science fiction writers, but they can also be daunting. At this stage, it only has to make sense to you. If you're writing a story that takes place in more than one country, I highly suggest making a map before you start writing. Going back and having to painstakingly make minute changes in many places because you miscalculated the distance from one place to another will make you want to gouge your eyes out.

Okay, maybe not *that* drastic, but it isn't fun.

Your map doesn't have to be pretty. My husband laughs at my maps (I can barely draw stick figures; it's pretty pathetic). And then he re-draws them and they look fantastic.

So what should your map include?

A graphical scale

A *what*, you say? These are those tiny measuring sticks on maps that say how many inches/centimeters equal a certain amount of miles/kilometers/however you're measuring distance.

It doesn't matter if your fictional world uses a different scale of measurement than you use, whether fictional or real. There must be some way to reliably measure distances from place to place on your map.

You'll thank me later when you don't have to rewrite the timing of any traveling in your story, or completely redraw your map.

Natural boundaries

Mountain ranges

Canyons

Forests

Deserts

Coasts/shorelines

Water sources

Oceans

Lakes

Rivers

Springs & aquifers – where there are trees, there is water, whether on the surface or underground.

Make sure to note whether a body of water is freshwater or saltwater. If your characters are human, they *must* have access to fresh water for survival, whether it is straight from the source, filtered, or distilled.

Man-made boundaries

Giant walls – think Great Wall of China.

Symbolic boundaries – the borders of states, countries, empires, etc.

Major roads

Ruins – especially of castles, major roads, fortresses, etc.

Major cities

Capital cities

Large ports

Major production sites – such as rock quarries or mines.

Large trading posts – these will be more remote, but near intersections of major travel routes.

All of these will be clumped around major water sources, or very near to them, so put those on your map before doing this.

Anything vital to your story.

Camp sites

Battle sites

The location of the Thing The Entire Plot Hinges On – like a volcano where you have to dispose of a magic ring.

Your character's home

Anything else you think of

Many of these you may have to mark on your maps as you go along, but do as much as you know now.

Other Inspiration

If you're stumped about what climate or terrain would be best for your story, pull out a world atlas. Look for regions that are similar to what you have in mind, and look up the history and geography of them.

Not everything on *your* map will end up on the final map for your readers. Make sure that it's legible and you can understand your own markings. Don't worry about how pretty it is yet.

Old maps are really fun, especially the *really* old ones that have mysterious markings or 'Here be monsters' and such. Let them spark your imagination!

'Geography' Exercises

1. Briefly describe the area your character is from.

Where is their nearest source of water? What kind of terrain do they see when they look outside? What is the climate like?

2. What was the last major change to that terrain within your character's lifetime? If there has been no change in their lifetime, what was the most recent change?

A flash flood is as simple as it needs to be to reroute a stream, or wipe out a road. An earthquake would have to be pretty major to cause serious, permanent changes to the terrain, though, and it would severely damage or destroy any town that might be on the site.

The A-Zs of Worldbuilding

3. What does your character's country look like? Is it large enough to contain more than one climate, or does it fit inside a single climate region?

Are there plains, forests, deserts? What are the main bodies of water accessible to the people there – rivers, lakes, or an ocean? Are the borders symbolic, based on treaty lines? Or are they natural, like a mountain range or coast?

_____
_____
_____
_____
_____
_____
_____
_____
_____
_____

4. Are there different laws of nature in your world than in ours? Why? What changes?

Do you have a random snowy forest right next to a hot desert? How would that work in your world? Is there too much rain near or in a desert area? Or a blizzard on the equator?

_____
_____
_____
_____
_____
_____
_____
_____
_____
_____

5. Use the space below to draw a simple map of the world you have described so far.

Remember: It doesn't have to be pretty! Just functional. Don't bother with cities yet, just get down what the region looks like (coastlines, rivers and lakes, forests, plains, etc.), your compass points, and what the graphical scale measurements are. Keep the graphical scale simple, using measurement terms you understand easily.

6. Now that you've drawn a map, we're going to fill it in just a bit more. What natural resources might be found, both visible and not, that can be harvested for use?

Visible resources will be things like trees (for lumber), possible quarries, the grazing grounds of animals that can be hunted, native medicinal plants, water springs, etc. Non-visible resources will be veins of ore that can be mined, underground aquifers (water reservoirs), etc.

_____
_____
_____
_____
_____
_____
_____
_____
_____
_____

7. What are existing landmarks?

These may be geographic anomalies (like a mountain range with a specific amount of peaks, or even shaped like something else – perhaps a dragon's spine or someone lying on their side), or sites of historic or religious importance. The terrain may have even been altered because of historic or religious events, and that is how the area is identified.

_____
_____
_____
_____
_____
_____
_____
_____

8. What cultural regions exist?

Where have people settled, and why? Tie some of this into any historic or religious landmarks you have decided on. Settled regions that are quite a ways apart may also result in different subcultures and dialects of a region's main culture and language.

9. What are the important cities and towns?

How were they settled and established? What are the cities that contain seats of government, such as the reigning monarchs, a parliament, or perhaps a federal treasury or major military base?

10. What geography resources are you using?

G is for Geography

H is for History
The Past Shapes the Future

History is very important, especially in speculative fiction. The plots of many fantasy and science fiction stories hinge on either the knowledge or ignorance of past events. History will affect your story at two levels – characterization and plot.

"Those who cannot remember the past are condemned to repeat it."
George Santayana

You don't need to know every little intricacy of the history of your world, but there are a few vital things you need to figure out.

One of the easiest ways to begin is by looking at where your story starts. If you have some semblance of a plot in place already, you will probably have the inciting incidents figured out.

Inciting Incident: the encounter that sets your story's conflict in motion.

If the inciting incident is something more than a personal conflict, then it will likely be something that belongs in your world's history. There are some kinds of personal conflict that may change history, though, such as a disagreement between monarchs which causes a breakdown in *all* relations between factions.

Conflict does not mean a fight or argument, in this context.
Rather, it is what brings forced change into your character's life.

Once you know where your story starts, you can start tracing backwards into history. Every historical event has a start somewhere, and sometimes in the most innocuous of places. Ancient family feuds can easily turn into major wars, perhaps even years after the feud started, simply because someone somewhere along the way passed the feud on to their progeny, and/or forgot what the feud was about in the first place and it just kept going because *that's how things were.*

If you've made a map that covers the area of your fictional country or world, take a moment to pull that map out and look at where valuable resources might be located. Anything on the border between countries, or anything vital for survival, might be something that could cause a war if one nation decides to claim total control.

Really, though, wars are usually not complicated when it comes down to the initial inciting incident. It doesn't have to be sane, either. There just needs to be a reason, even if that reason only makes sense to the person(s) responsible.

Make sure to note how you *currently* think the plot of your story is going to affect the *future* of the inhabitants of your fictional world. You're not setting this in concrete, but it will help you keep your writing and characterization consistent if you have a known goal you're working toward.

Create a Timeline

Timelines are your lifesaver when it comes to intricate plots with historical significance.

It can be as simple or as complex as you like, as long as it makes sense to you. There are several different software options available, but you can also pull out paper and pen (or pencil), index cards, or just make a bullet list in a document on your computer, whatever method works best for you.

Your timeline should include:

Birth and (if applicable) death dates for the characters in your story.

> Trust me, there's really nothing worse than thinking your characters have first-hand knowledge of an event, then realizing that event happened before they were born, or after they died.

Events that directly affect your characters.

> Historical events that directly affect your character, either because the event has direct repercussions in their life, or because they witnessed it.

> Localized events that have less historical bearing, but could still be off-shoots of historical events.

> Events which may not be historically significant at all but have drastically shaped who your character is. A seemingly innocent remark can change someone's course in life if it is said at the right – or wrong – time. Conversely, something that might be a significant event for someone else may not be a defining moment for your character.

Events that directly affect your plot.

> Any wars, famines, natural disasters, etc. that have happened in your characters' lifetimes, or have repercussions that reach into their lifetimes. This can also include positive events – a long period of peace, several years of especially abundant harvests, etc.

> Anything that actually happens in your story that is a major event. The first time your character tries seafood probably doesn't count – unless, of course, your character is royalty and happens to be allergic to seafood.

Events that affect how your characters lands came to exist.

> These are political events, treaties, declarations of war, the discovery of resources, etc. It could also be the founding of a religion, a major technological invention, or the establishment of the ruling power. *Anything* that shapes the current culture.

Other Inspiration

Human motivations don't change much, if at all. So, if you're really stumped, look at actual history. I cannot tell you how many stories I've read where the author states in an introduction that the story is just a retelling of *such and such* war – the War of the Roses is a *very* popular one, though, so you might want to try and find a different source. There are plenty of wars in recorded history to choose from!

'History' Exercises

1. What historical events happened to enable the inciting incident of your story?

This doesn't have to be detailed yet, but get the basic picture down of which people and/or countries are involved, and how. Did these events happen before or after your main character was born?

2. What historical events have most impacted the cultures of your world?

These can be a wide range of possibilities. A plague may influence how a country is governed, depending on how many live and die. Genocide may completely change a culture – both the victims and the perpetrators. Treaties and wars will bring in elements of other cultures that may be assimilated over time.

The A-Zs of Worldbuilding

3. How long has your character's country and/or people group existed?
Have they recently established themselves and their culture is still forming, or do they have years and years of traditions in place?

_____
_____
_____
_____
_____
_____
_____
_____
_____
_____

4. What is the oldest country or people group in your world?
They may or may not be a 'superpower,' but they will probably be a formidable threat to any newer countries or cultures.

_____
_____
_____
_____
_____
_____
_____
_____
_____

5. What is the newest country or culture in your world?

They will probably not be a superpower, but they will likely be perceived as a threat by the older regimes.

6. What are the historical events that have most impacted who your character is?

Regardless of the story, what has affected your character the most, and shaped their personality and morals? Whether this is witnessing the start of a war, surviving a plague, or even possibly being at the right place at the right time to not be affected by a major tragedy.

The A-Zs of Worldbuilding

7. Make a brief timeline of the events pertaining directly to your inciting incident.

Try to stay within 5-10 years prior to your inciting incident. Don't go very far past the inciting incident into the future, either. Just get the bare details down.

8. What resources are you using from our world to help create the history of yours?

I is for Interior Design
Setting the Indoor Atmosphere

It's not creepy if you like to poke through your fictional character's bedroom, right? Well, so be it if it is, because I have found that one of the best ways to learn about where a person comes from and what they are like is to look inside their bedroom.

However, we aren't focusing on character building as much in this workbook, but rather worldbuilding. So we're going to look at *what* is in the bedroom (or really, any rooms) versus why your character picked those things specifically.

Culture & Lifestyle

Culture greatly influences homes and how people decorate them. In America, we have quite a mash-up of styles because of immigration, but there are still a lot of things that are common in many homes. Some examples would be pictures or posters on the walls, curtains on the windows, video game consoles and game or DVD collections, photo albums, sofas and recliners, etc. Think those aren't cultural? Think again. Most of the world does not have those things, except in *some* more developed nations – it's a *first world culture* thing.

Much of this varies by income level – our modern equivalent of social status. The items mentioned in the previous paragraph are a few examples: while most of that is *common*, there are a few things that are almost always found in every home, regardless of income level. Televisions, video game consoles, video game/DVD collections, and a sofa or recliner. This is because our culture is very entertainment-oriented.

How your people live will influence quite a bit of how they decorate. Income level will dictate it the most, but even the poorest people will usually find some way to decorate and add cheer wherever or however they happen to be residing.

The busier the lifestyle they have, though, the less likely they are to have a lot of *stuff*, unless they make enough money to pay someone to take care of their stuff. Peasants will have minimal decoration, both because of income and because they have a hard enough time just making sure there is food to put on the table on a semi-regular basis. They're not going to worry about dusting knick-knacks, too. Wealthier classes have more things because, for one example, they don't have to care for it all by themselves.

There are also practical reasons for how a home is decorated. Take curtains, for example. Beyond adding color and decoration to a room, curtains offer a further element of privacy than bare windows do. They also help block drafts and excess light. If glass does not exist in your world, there may be oiled parchment in the windows, or just open frames with shutters.

If a culture is very religious, there may be design elements that have incorporated themselves specifically for the reason of being ritualistic reminders. The Jewish *mezuzah* is one example. It doesn't just have to be something that affixes to a doorframe or wall, though. It could be charms and talismans spread about the home for luck, or to ward off spirits. Perhaps even the shape of doors and windows has evolved from a superstition.

Mezuzah are small decorative cases, containing portions of scripture, which affix to doorframes.

I is for Interior Design

Now if you've stuck all of your characters in spaceships for the duration of your story, there will be some limitations to how much they can alter their living space, but you can bet there will be some elements of home that they make sure are around them. Unless, of course, spaceships *are* home and the basis of their culture.

Other Inspiration

Once again, look around you. Look at design elements you like, and the cultures behind them (when applicable) and let it spark your imagination. You're writing speculative fiction – the possibilities are endless!

'Interior Design' Exercises

1. Is there an item or room that is in every home, regardless of social status?

Think shrines, talismans, and conveniences that have become commonplace – like bathrooms.

_____
_____
_____
_____
_____
_____
_____
_____
_____

2. What types of weather frequently need to be kept out of the homes? How is it done both efficiently, and beautifully?

If a climate is hot, there needs to be plenty of ventilation. Cold climates will have a variety of ways to help keep warm – whether it is stacks of furs to use, or wood stoves nestled in every room.

_____
_____
_____
_____
_____
_____
_____
_____
_____

3. What resources are available for creating decorative items in homes?

Any resource that is available in abundance will become a cultural trademark, such as a specific pigment for dyes and paints (crushed shells, dried and crushed insects, or even leaves and berries can all be used as pigment or dye), or specific fibers that are used for decorative textiles, etc.

___

4. Briefly describe a peasant home.

Think minimal and functional, but still with some personalized touches here and there. Items most likely to be personalized are things that have to be handmade.

The A-Zs of Worldbuilding

5. Briefly describe a middle-class home.
Think 'merchants.' They might have some harder-to-find items in their homes, but not necessarily expensive ones.

6. Briefly describe a wealthy home.
These will be larger, with more furnishings and rooms, because they are able to hire help. Expensive, rare items will be more likely to be found in these homes, too. Even commonplace items will be better quality, and possibly fancied up.

7. What types of decorations are found in every home, but made of different materials depending on cost?
These might be beds, seating, fireplaces, stoves and ovens, etc.

8. What type of décor will appear for holidays or special events?
This might be certain colors of candles, decorative coverings for shrines or altars, greenery brought inside during the coldest parts of the year, etc.

9. What are your interior design resources?

I is for Interior Design

J is for Judicial Systems
Establishing Law & Order

I'll be honest. I never thought about judicial systems in fantasy until I started on one particular story, and found myself writing a courtroom drama. I suddenly needed to know a lot more about the laws and judicial processes of the world I was working in.

Sometimes there's no way to predict what you will need from your worldbuilding when you sit down to start your first draft, but that is part of why I'm doing this workbook. If you have at least the bare bones figured out, if it turns out you need *more*, you'll already have a foundation to work from, and it won't throw you off track as much.

You may want to refer back to the *E is for Economy*[5] for some of this. The hierarchy between the economic system and the judicial system are often connected, if they aren't the same.

We will be covering more about the actual structure of government in *Q is for Queens*[6], and often the structure of the judicial system is intertwined with that, so if you need to skip ahead and work on that, or delay working on this chapter until you've gone through the workbook a little more, that's fine.

Authority

Judicial authority will vary some based on the type of government in control. A monarchy will hold all final authority, unless their powers have been limited. In some places, the branch of government that creates laws is not directly responsible for enforcing them, either.

Jurisdiction

Some offenses may be dealt with at local levels by townships or states (for example, theft from a local merchant, or the murder of civilians within certain regions). There may be other crimes that are dealt with higher up in the level of authority, though. A spy may face charges of treason and be subject to sentencing by the reigning monarch.

Maintaining Order

Some laws, codes, and taxes will be easy to maintain, especially those that the common people feel are beneficial to maintain order in society. No one likes to have something stolen from them, so for the most part this type of law will be self-enforced. Everyone likes safe, sturdy roads too, so taxes for things like that will be more amenable to the people.

Others will be harder to maintain, though. Newly imposed taxes or tributes (especially when citizens or subjects are already strained for resources) may require penalties and threats to be effectively enforced.

Other Inspiration

Look at political science textbooks – they are awesome for giving inspiration about judicial systems. Feel free to pick elements from different types of judicial systems, too, and manipulate them to work within your world and story.

---

[5] E is for Economy, pg. 36
[6] Q is for Queens, pg. 150

'Judicial Systems' Exercises

1. Who is responsible for creating laws?

Are laws created on the local level, the national level, or a combination of both?

2. Who is responsible for enforcing them?

Does a local police force do this, or the army?

The A-Zs of Worldbuilding

3. Is there a criminal justice system in place? How does it work?
What happens when someone is accused of a crime? Is there a trial? Who oversees it?

4. Are different branches of government responsible for different aspects of the law?
One branch of government may be responsible for crimes against the state, another for crimes against individuals, etc.

5. How much of the law is handled at the local level, and how much at the state/province and/or national level?

Would local law enforcement be allowed to handle charges of treason, for example, or would they have to defer to higher authority?

6. What are the most basic laws your society follows?

What is considered to be common courtesy that may be supported by the legal system, but is typically self-enforced?

The A-Zs of Worldbuilding

7. How long have those laws been around?
Were these laws put into place with the establishment of the governing force, or have they been around since before that?

___

8. Are those laws still followed, or are they considered to be archaic?
What of those are cultural laws that may have changed or become obsolete as society changed and grew? What laws are currently still enforced, but may be considered out-of-date by the people?

9. What resources are you using to create your judicial systems?

K is for Knowledge
Understanding the World

What does knowledge have to do with worldbuilding?

Well, knowledge is, essentially, the accumulation of information. The information accumulated has everything to do with how a culture and society grow.

Information and knowledge are how we understand everything around us, at least to an extent. Humans will never know everything about everything. 'Everything' is simply too vast for that to be possible.

There are three ways a society deals with knowledge:

>They *encourage* the pursuit of it.
>
>They *allow* the pursuit of it.
>
>Or, they actively *forbid* the accumulation of it.

So what does this mean for your worldbuilding? How a society deals with knowledge can be a key indicator of how they govern.

A society which actively supports the pursuit of knowledge is a society that isn't afraid of its people. Information may still be biased because authors will see things differently, but the flow of knowledge in and out of the society will be massive. It will both be harder and easier to hide things, depending on how diligent people are in searching for truth.

A society that allows the pursuit of knowledge, but with constraints, wants the illusion of complete freedom. Constraints are such things as censoring, saying no without actually saying no, and making full knowledge only available to a privileged few.

When an oppressive government comes into power, one of the first things they do is restrict knowledge. Intelligent people – especially ones in positions of authority, such as professors, teachers, doctors, and clergy – are targeted. The government's agenda is to spread their own versions of, well, *everything*. They will actively destroy knowledge that contradicts their agenda. It can start with simple methods – restricting access to knowledge and flooding the information pathways with propaganda. When that doesn't work, and sometimes as they gain more control, this can become anything from book burning, to brainwashing, to people disappearing if they've said the wrong thing.

***Propaganda** is biased, sometimes fictional, information made to look like fact, specifically for the purpose of swaying people's opinions. Propaganda is not always spread or commissioned by the government.*

The specific actions the governing authorities do take will be based on *why* they are limiting knowledge. Are they doing so because they're trying to hide information about a specific event (or events), potentially for the perceived good of the public? Or are they limiting knowledge to maintain complete control of the people?

Overall, *how* the government deals with knowledge will affect every walk of life within society. It will change how characters and their intentions are perceived, especially if they think the government is to blame for any or all hardships.

Ultimately, it will change how characters react to laws, to each other, and to circumstances outside their control. Especially if they feel they might have handled something better if they'd only *known*.

Other Inspiration

Sadly, human history is rife with examples of how governments dealt poorly with knowledge. Current events in many places are also good examples of this, and there simply aren't many examples of governments handling 'free' knowledge well. It doesn't mean that it can't work in your world. Just remember: characters are supposed to be flawed, so there really isn't any such thing as the perfect society, no matter how much knowledge is at their disposal.

The A-Zs of Worldbuilding

'Knowledge' Exercises

1. How much does each culture know?

The lifestyle and priorities of each culture will affect the type of knowledge they value, and how deeply they've pursued it. Some of it will be because of necessity – like medical knowledge. A world that hasn't known disease will know very little about treating illness. Don't forget to consider knowledge of divinity/theology/spiritualism if your culture is religious or had religious roots.

_____
_____
_____
_____
_____
_____
_____
_____
_____

2. How technologically advanced are they?

How long have they had certain advancements? Is their knowledge in this area still growing? Does their technology facilitate the sharing of knowledge in anyway?

_____
_____
_____
_____
_____
_____
_____
_____
_____

3. How do they store information?

Is knowledge passed down orally, or is there a written language? Are there any specific ways that your cultures pass down knowledge, such as the direct transfer of memories from one person to another? What about storing information with technology, such as flash drives?

_____
_____
_____
_____
_____
_____
_____
_____
_____
_____

4. What schooling options exist?

Are there publicly funded schools? Religious schools? Private schools, and/or private tutors? What about home education? What might be advantages, disadvantages, or hindrances for any of these options?

_____
_____
_____
_____
_____
_____
_____
_____
_____
_____

The A-Zs of Worldbuilding

5. Is any type of schooling mandatory for all people? Is there a minimum amount of schooling required? If not, how far does the average person go through school?

Keep in mind that the priority of this may change based on other factors. Hands-on knowledge may be valued much more highly than 'book knowledge' if growing food is necessary for survival.

_____
_____
_____
_____
_____
_____
_____
_____
_____

6. Are there any types of higher education available?

In some places, this may be an apprenticeship. In others, it may be hours spent in a classroom (or multiple classrooms) learning specific things before being allowed to practice, such as certain sciences (medicine, chemistry, etc.) Further experience may be required as well.

_____
_____
_____
_____
_____
_____
_____
_____
_____

7. Do any specific institutions for higher learning exist? Who runs them?

Universities are fairly universal – they show up everywhere. Both in real life and in speculative fiction. But they are not mandatory, and often access to them may be limited by more than just being 'smart enough.' Social (not income) status may also hinder or permit one to attend university.

8. Are there any incentives offered for accruing knowledge?

Perhaps guaranteed jobs, or improved social status. It can also be as simple as the prestige an individual may acquire for certain levels of achievements (a masters or PhD), or acquiring the knowledge from a certain place or person (such as an Ivy League college or a famous guru).

The A-Zs of Worldbuilding

9. Are there any government authorities actively involved in the curation of knowledge?
If knowledge is nationally valued, there is a very good chance that those in authority will sponsor different things. Examples would be art funding, or patrons.

10. Are there any limitations on what information is accessible to the common people? How is it explained?
Think about whether information may need to be classified (because of security risk), or it might just vanish. A pay wall (subscription fees, for example) can also be an effective way of making information inaccessible to certain groups.

11. Does the government take an active role in spreading knowledge, or is it left up to individuals?
Public schooling. Public service announcements. Government-sponsored continuing education, etc.

12. Does the government actively prohibit certain types of information?
Is anything censored? Why? This is different than the concepts in question 10, because anyone can limit access to knowledge they control. Censorship would control even knowledge with limited-access, and alter public knowledge.

13. What resources are you using from our world for information about knowledge in your world?

L is for Language
A Brief Overview of Language Construction

There is much potential in speculative fiction for fictional languages, but it is not mandatory to create a language at all. Tolkien did so, yes, but Tolkien did so because he was fascinated with linguistics long before he sat down to finalize his stories. He *taught* linguistics as a profession.

I am not, by any means, a linguistic expert. I enjoy creating languages, but there is so much of it that is over my head. It is not possible for me to cover the extent of this on my own.

There is, however, an excellent resource for creating fictional languages: *The Language Construction Kit*[7]

I found *The Language Construction Kit* several years ago, and it has proven to be an invaluable resource time and time again. All their information is available for free on their website, or you can choose to order it as an e-book, or a print book.

I won't blame you if you want to skip my section altogether and use *The Language Construction Kit* instead. However, if you want a light version of creating a language, please continue!

The Basics of Communication & Interaction

Communication is the basis of human relationship and interaction. Societies and cultures are built around this interaction, and language develops from there. But language is so much more than *just* the spoken words – it is context, slang, implications, metaphor and simile, and hyperbole.

Languages will form in a common area, but as people spread out, dialects will develop, and eventually if a group is isolated from the 'mother' language for long enough, a dialect may turn into its own language.

It is easiest to start with words first, rather than creating an alphabet. An alphabet for a spoken language never really comes into play until a written language is recorded.

If a language is a derivative of another one, you'll need to have a few root words for the base language first, unless the mother language won't be referred to at all in your story.

Use similar sounds from word to word, and keep your root words simple. They don't need to have more than three syllables.

Once you have your root words, you can derive words from them. The word for 'rain' might come from the root word for 'water', for example. 'Light' and 'fire' might be related to each other. 'Speak' and 'sing,' etc.

When you have about 10-15 words down (using whatever alphabet is your normal one – *do not* worry about creating a fictional written alphabet yet), look at what sounds and *types* of sounds (hard sounds, soft sounds, guttural sounds, etc.) you've used the most. Use those as a way to make your language sound unique.

---

[7] http://www.zompist.com/kit.html

> *Hard sounds* mostly pertain to 'c' and 'g' in English. A hard c sounds like a k. Soft c sounds more like an s. A hard or soft g is like 'goat' and 'gelatin', respectively.
>
> *Soft sounds* are what most vowels and consonants are by default, in English.
>
> *Guttural* sounds are practically non-existent in English. The closest thing would be a hard 'g' sound. German and Hebrew are examples of guttural languages.

If you're a complete nerd (like me) and might actually be speaking this language (even if you're just mumbling to yourself about your story), keep things so that the human mouth and throat are capable of pronouncing them.

The Written Language

Creating an alphabet is like creating a written code, and this is part of the reason you shouldn't mess with it right at the beginning. It's never fun to try and go back and figure out what you were saying in a language when you've lost your alphabet.

When creating an alphabet, keep in mind the type of materials available for writing. No one is going to develop a delicate flowing alphabet if they have to chisel everything. It's going to start off with the simplest, straightest lines possible. Over time, it can become more delicate and cursive-like, but it's always going to have remnants of what it originally was.

Keep in mind that you will need vowels and consonants, or a way to 'turn' consonants into vowels. One example is Hebrew, where consonants have vowel markers instead of separate letters that are vowels.

Other Inspiration

Languages are vast in our world, and if you are looking for something with a specific sort of sound, there's a chance it already exists and you may just need to do some digging for inspiration.

Do *not* rip off entire existing languages for your story (dead languages will have less restrictions), but do feel free to find inspiration from them, and even use your work as a way to bring awareness of other cultures to your readers. When possible, consult native speakers of the language as well. There are many nuances that can be missed otherwise.

Don't get so caught up in creating a language – or worldbuilding in general – that you get frustrated or distracted from your true purpose for all of this: writing your story.

You just need to write your story, whether it requires a fictional language or not.

'Language' Exercises

1. Look at your people groups. How many are there, and how much distance is between them?

Are they related to each other? How long has it been since they were a single group?

_____
_____
_____
_____
_____
_____
_____
_____

2. How long have their languages been developing?

Which languages started at the same time, but in separate parts of the world? Which ones have branched off from a mother tongue, but ultimately ended up as their own unique languages? What about dialects within languages?

_____
_____
_____
_____
_____
_____
_____
_____

3. What are 5-7 root words of your 'mother' tongue?
Basic words. Likely things that were important in day-to-day life.

4. What are 10-15 more words, derived from those root words?
These can be very literal, or very abstract.

The A-Zs of Worldbuilding

5. What sounds did you use the most?

Hard sounds, soft sounds, guttural sounds? What were the exact sounds?

6. Look at the words you've compiled so far. Decide if your written language will have vowels, or consonants with vowel markers.

If you have a lot of vowels, then having actual letters to represent them may be easier. If there are only a few vowels, then consonants with vowel markers may be more convenient.

7. How many letters are there in total?

If you use consonants with vowel markers, you can get away with fewer letters overall.

8. What does your alphabet look like?

I recommend using a pencil for this part! Make your letters cohesive, but not too similar. You need to be able to tell the letters apart without too much difficulty.

9. How do people interact with each other?
What are the social norms for conversation?

10. What phrases or sayings are considered rude?
You know, what do you never *say in polite company?*

11. What type of slang exists?

It always exists. Unless the culture is very literal about everything.

12. What are traditional greetings and farewells?

This may tie in with religious beliefs, or be a simple hello and goodbye. Refer also to the Xenial exercises (pg. 222).

13. What are your language resources?

L is for Language

M is for Military
Armies, Soldiers, and Tactics

Speculative fiction often falls into one of two extremes: you either have wars (or countries on the verge of war, or civil wars, etc.) or... you have peace-loving, tree-hugging hippies.

No offense to hippies of any stripe. I'm almost one myself.

There is definitely a happy medium to be found, but unless your fictional people groups are literally *perfect*, there will be conflict. There will be crimes. There will be wars. And there will be senseless deaths.

Defense and offense are the two main things a military force will deal with.

You will need to decide, though, if your country keeps a standing army during peacetime, or if soldiers are conscripted as needed when conflict arrives. There is also the option of keeping a military force in reserve, so that soldiers are already trained when they are required. When a reserve force is not an option and the need for soldiers arises, mercenaries may be hired. This depends on whether there is enough funds for that, of course.

How large an army needs to be depends on how much force could be brought against them, how large their country actually is (more borders means more soldiers, because there is simply more area to cover), and what the population is like. Some of it may also depend on how spread out the population is – it takes fewer soldiers to protect one city, for example, versus several cities or towns spread over a vast distance.

You will also need to take into consideration the technology available. The training and tactics in a fight will be vastly different if it needs to be hand-to-hand combat, or if they have long-range weapons of any sort.

I recommend figuring out the basics of the command structure within your armed forces, as well. It's just one of those things, again, that makes it easier when you get into the actual writing. I've had to stop and figure out ranks and command structure in the middle of scenes before, and it's more than a little distracting to say the least.

Other Inspiration

Don't be afraid of picking up tactics books. *The Art of War* is one that is recommended often and reading it for yourself will not hurt your story. I would, however, caution against using it as blatant inspiration in your writing. It has been done many times, and if I had a dollar for every fantasy story I've read that makes mention of *The Art of War* or some thinly-disguised substitute, I'd be rich.

Books about war history are also a good place to start, though lengthier and more time consuming. Don't just study the tactics, but study the reasons behind the battles and the politics manipulating forces from behind the scenes.

Otherwise, feel free to use ranks and titles and command structure from existing military forces. They are fairly standard and easy for people to understand, just make sure they make sense within your fictional world.

'Military' Exercises

1. Do your people have any enemies? Why?

Family feud gone wrong? Limited access to resources? Differing opinions? All these are legitimate reasons for conflict between groups.

___

2. Who has something your people want?

A mine for gems? Fertile fields for growing food? Access to clean water?

3. What are they willing to do to get it?
Negotiations will likely come first, but sometimes in desperate circumstances, war may start prior to any bargaining.

4. What borders would need to be defended from invasion?
Some borders are more difficult to be crossed – like a coast line, or a mountain range. Others are easy. Flat plains, small rivers or creeks, etc.

5. Has an official military force been established? When?
Was it formed in anticipation of a situation, or after there was already a problem?

6. Who is allowed to enlist?
Are there any age, health, or gender restrictions? Why?

The A-Zs of Worldbuilding

7. How does enlistment work?

Is the process simple, or complicated? Does one simply show up the day of the battle, or do they have to register and pass any exams (health or otherwise)?

_____
_____
_____
_____
_____
_____
_____
_____
_____
_____

8. Is a standing army kept ready even during times of peace?

Who serves, and why? Is it mandatory for certain people to serve (members of the royalty may be required to command if the kingdom is at war), or completely voluntary?

_____
_____
_____
_____
_____
_____
_____
_____
_____
_____

9. How quickly can they respond to threats?

Think of the ancient Roman highways – they were built specifically to make great distances passable by their armies. Depending on the access your people have to certain materials, infrastructures like this are certainly feasible.

___

10. How technologically advanced is the military?

Clubs and stones? Bows and arrows? Automatic weapons? What sorts of weapons of mass destruction are at hand? Are there weaponized vehicles or aircraft?

The A-Zs of Worldbuilding

11. Is there standard equipment that is issued to soldiers? What about uniforms?

Some cultures, especially with limited resources, may require soldiers to provide their own equipment. More structured armed forces may require uniforms so that there is an appearance of unity. It may also help training and tactics flow more smoothly if everyone has the same equipment.

12. What types of transportation can they rely on?

Horse and cart? Teleportation magic? Space jets?

13. What is your military most well-known for?
Cavalry, infantry, scare tactics, using mercenaries, etc.

14. What was the first incident that required your people to defend their lives?
How did they deal with the situation? Did they have any armed forces at that point yet?

The A-Zs of Worldbuilding

15. What was their worst loss?

How did they deal with impossible odds? Or, how were they defeated in a battle they were certain they would win?

_____

_____

_____

_____

_____

_____

_____

_____

_____

16. What was their greatest victory?

Once again, impossible odds, or sure victory?

_____

_____

_____

_____

_____

_____

_____

_____

_____

17. What resources are you using from our world for your military worldbuilding?

N is for Nuptials
Marriage & Relationships in Fictional Cultures

We've talked about birth and death so far, and we'll deal with coming-of-age as well in this book[8], but let's take a moment to talk about marriage!

Marriage serves a role in society – it is a binding agreement between individuals for the purpose of creating a stable environment. That environment is used either for the purpose of rearing children, for a transfer of authority, or pooling assets.

There are other aspects of marriage as well, but they are less likely to impact a speculative fiction story so much that you need to worry about them before they happen in your story.

Sexuality

There could certainly be an entire section in this workbook for sexuality, but alas, it did not fit this time around. Sexuality will certainly affect marriages and relationships, though, so we will briefly discuss them in this section.

Same-sex relations and incest are some of the two most obvious situations that will need to be dealt with, especially the latter if you're modeling your world after our society at all.

Some cultures may fully embrace same-sex relationships. How you deal with same-sex relationships is up to you, just know that a culture or religion that views sex as an activity for procreation rather than pleasure will see same-sex issues as 'unnatural.' Reactions towards same-sex relationships can range from 'we just don't talk about this' to outright persecution and/or a death penalty for offenses.

Incest tends to be a quieter offense, if it is considered an offense by your fictional culture. There are plenty of examples of both types of relationships being either condoned or condemned in real-world history. Many places in the world today don't see a problem with cousins marrying cousins, even from the genetic side. The Egyptian dynasties intermarried sibling-to-sibling, for example, to keep the bloodlines pure, but without knowing the genetic devastation it would eventually cause.

Taboos (whether that is only discussing sexual matters with one of your own gender, or more extreme sexual tastes) would be an endless topic, especially since they are often not enforced by law, but rather by cultural preference. Sometimes the influence of a culture and its citizens can be greater than the force of the law, though, so consider that in your plotting.

Additionally, there is the option of asexuality (beyond the scientific term for asexual reproduction). This doesn't mean your character never has sex, but that sexual urges can be rare or non-existent. It is possible for asexuals to be in satisfying, long-term sexual relationships, and also for them to be happy without sexual relationships *ever*. Most importantly, don't box your characters in with stereotypes.

Sexuality can take an entirely different meaning in the case of some fictional universes where both genders can procreate in different ways, however.

---

[8] Y is for Youth, pg. 228

Ethics of Marriage

Marriage isn't something just anyone can up and do, or just randomly decide that they are married (most of the time, at least). Some considerations that need to be taken are the ages of the marrying parties, what local law or tradition dictates about who (or what, depending on your world) is allowed to marry, and what rights and/or assets are being exchanged.

Arranged marriages can be a whole different level of negotiation as well, especially if parents or guardians are not taking the feelings of who they are 'giving away' into consideration. Not all arranged marriages end badly, though.

In many cultures, arranged marriage is considered normal, if not the majority. Orthodox Jews usually only speak with their intended spouse a few times before determining if they are compatible and will enter into marriage. Usually, the intended is someone their parents think will get along with them. Many cultures in Asia and the Middle East practice arranged marriages to this day.

Legality

There are a few different ways you can deal with the legal side of marriage in your worlds.

Civil unions

A marriage put on record with the governing authorities, but no other documentation, witnessing, or vow-taking is required.

Holy matrimony

It may not be called holy matrimony in your world, but in essence it would be the same: the belief that the validity of a marriage doesn't come from the government's endorsement of it, but from vows taken before a deity.

Holy matrimony is often considered more binding than a marriage dictated by contract law. It is often considered to be a covenant.

Covenants are, in their most simple form, an agreement to do or not do something. In modern legality, covenants are part of what makes up a legally binding contract. Covenants can exist outside of a contract, however. They are not legally binding in that case, though in ancient societies a covenant would have been more binding than a signed contract. A covenant was often guaranteed by the lives of the two agreeing to the covenant.

Common-law marriage

A couple living together for enough time to be considered married by the governing authorities, despite never having documented the marriage with them or with a place of worship.

Handfasting

A trial marriage, in a sense. The intended couple lives together for a specific amount of time (usually a year and a day), to see if they could actually make their relationship work long-term. If, at the end of the trial period, they wish to remain together, they are considered to have been married for that time. If they wish to part ways, it's basically no harm/no foul.

Going 'outside' of a marriage

Depending on the laws and beliefs governing marriage, extramarital affairs may be a subject that characters have to deal with in your world.

There can be many nuances to these types of affairs. If having someone on the side is a cultural tradition, then it may be something that either (or both) spouses are prepared to deal with. Someone marrying into that culture, though, may be quite shocked.

You will need to take laws of inheritance into consideration, especially in the case of potentially illegitimate offspring. And there may be sexually transmitted diseases to be aware of as well.

Polyamory

Polyamory is when at least three people are engaged in an intimate, romantic relationship together. In a culture or society that only recognizes marriage between two people (whether of the same or opposite sex), there are many issues that could arise, especially regarding custody and inheritance rights for any offspring.

Polygamy

Polygamy is the practice of one person with many spouses, and there are many ways this can play out. There could be concubines, where the first wife has all power between the husband/wife relationship, and the additional wives have lesser status (you can flip those roles around too – one wife with many husbands). Perhaps all spouses have to agree on a potential future spouse, as well. Since there are not romantic or sexual relationships between additional spouses (unless it is a polyamorous, polygamous marriage), there can be added issues of jealousy between spouses. And as we know by now, conflict means story potential!

Marriage & Wedding Traditions

This is where it gets fun!

How do couples court each other?

It can be subtle or blatant, but it will be affected by other aspects of the culture. If women are not considered full members of society, they may have very little say in who they get to accept or refuse. And there may not be much wooing involved at all.

Conversely, you might have a culture where the woman has the complete say and can turn down a suitor for any reason, and that's just how it has to be.

As for actual courtship rituals, there could be dating-type scenarios, arranged marriages where the members never actually meet until the wedding, or long drawn-out activities where the couple has to overcome a certain number of challenges to prove that they are a good match and can sustain a relationship.

What happens at a wedding?

The main event is, of course, the vows those involved actually take. There is usually a celebration and/or feast that takes place as well, sometimes before the exchanging of vows and sometimes after, depending on cultural traditions. The ceremony might be followed by a honeymoon.

> *Honeymoon is used to refer to either the period of time just after a wedding, when the new couple is still freshly in love, or to the time they take away from their families and responsibilities to foster that bond.*

Depending on the nuances of a society, a wedding may be elaborate or casual, or it can be either one of those based on personal preference.

The main things you should figure out before having a wedding in your story is what is considered necessary and/or unacceptable at a wedding.

If there is a certain dress code for a wedding, clothing customs will have some say in this. If you've chosen a particular color or style of clothing to be associated with mourning, it will most certainly *not* be used at a wedding, except maybe in certain extreme circumstances. Examples might be: a sudden wedding where one of the participants has been recently widowed, the death of a figurehead in a society that dictates *everyone* must mourn when a monarch passes, etc.

Tokens are often exchanged to symbolize the vows, and in most modern societies now those would be wedding rings. However, it doesn't have to be rings. It can be some other sort of jewelry, or it could be something that takes a more visceral meaning – one may bring a sword, and the other a horse. These may be what they are best at using as a means of provision, or the items may literally be what means most to them in the world, and they are pledging those things to each other.

Some cultures also don't consider a marriage valid (or a wedding over) until there has been proof of the consummation of the wedding vows. Take that and run (er, write) as you will!

Other Inspiration

Look at historical weddings of different cultures. White has only been considered a wedding color in Western society for about two hundred years – we have Queen Victoria to thank for that trend. There are beautiful customs in other countries as well – a particular one is *mehendi*, the elaborate, gorgeous henna art done in India for a bride. Think outside the box. You never know what may strike your inspiration with beautiful sentimentality.

'Nuptials' Exercises

1. What laws and customs govern marriage?

Is there an age of consent? Who/what is allowed to marry, and why? Are arranged marriages allowed? Is it expected to be lifelong, or even last after death?

_____

2. What authority oversees marriage?

Is it a civil union, a religious one, or a combination of both? Or neither?

_____

3. How strict are any laws that govern the initiation of a marriage, and who enforces them?

Does a wedding ceremony have to be performed by certain authorities to be valid? What are some of the consequences that might be imposed for breaking the law?

_____
_____
_____
_____
_____
_____
_____
_____
_____
_____

4. Do common-law marriages exist?

What are the criteria for a common-law marriage? This is often a relationship having been in place for a certain amount of years, including cohabitation, and is recognized as a marriage by default. There could be a clause about needing a certain amount of assets to be shared in common, as well.

_____
_____
_____
_____
_____
_____
_____
_____

The A-Zs of Worldbuilding

5. Is handfasting accepted in place of, or as a predecessor for, a marriage?
If so, what are the common terms/conditions for a handfasting in your culture?

_____
_____
_____
_____
_____
_____
_____
_____

6. In the case of arranged marriages, what is permitted, and what are the rights of each party involved?
Are parents allowed to make betrothals on behalf of their not-of-age children? Are there legal protections in place for minors in that situation? What about for couples that are of age? Are marriages arranged by a religious figurehead, or even the government?

_____
_____
_____
_____
_____
_____
_____
_____
_____

7. Are there any laws that have bearing on extramarital affairs?

Is an extramarital affair viewed as a breach of contract (with divorce as a possible outcome) or a breach of covenant (with death as a possible punishment)?

___

8. Are there any laws or cultural taboos concerning sexuality?

Incest, same-sex relationships, interracial marriages, etc. Incest can take many forms: sibling/sibling, parent/child, aunts or uncles and their nieces or nephews, cousin/cousin, etc. Some of these may not be considered incest in some cultures – particularly cousin/cousin.

The A-Zs of Worldbuilding

9. Is there a time of courtship, dating, or wooing before a proposal of marriage?
This can be as simple as a dinner together, or as complex as a ritualistic dance.

10. Are there any specific traditions associated with betrothal and marriage?
The payment of a dowry, exchanging rings, 'something old, something new,' etc.

11. How differently do religions treat wedding ceremonies, or is there one cultural standard?

There may be a core standard that fits into them all, but is handled differently. A Catholic wedding, Protestant wedding, or Jewish wedding all have similarities, but are also vastly different.

12. Is there a traditional meal involved?

Feasting is an important part of celebrations in many cultures. The food served can also have symbolic meaning.

The A-Zs of Worldbuilding

13. Is the consummation of the marriage required for the marriage to have legal standing?

How is this witnessed? Does the wedding bed literally take center stage, or is it only necessary to display a bloody sheet? What if there is no virgin blood?

_____
_____
_____
_____
_____
_____
_____
_____

14. What about a honeymoon?

In some cultures, the time a couple spends secluded together immediately following marriage is considered vital. In others, life just goes on as usual – especially in places where inhabitants must continually work to ensure survival.

_____
_____
_____
_____
_____
_____
_____
_____

15. What resources are you using for developing nuptial traditions and laws in your world?

O is for Oblectation
The Pleasures of Life

Oblectation, according to The Phrontistery[9], means: enjoyment; pleasure.

Where there are people, there will be entertainment. Almost every facet of life is affected by how much enjoyment or pleasure can be derived from it. Pleasure is second only to survival.

How much and what kinds of recreation are available will depend on a person's lifestyle, and their wealth. For those with less money, going to a play or taking a vacation may not be a reasonable means of enjoyment, but reading a book or spending time outdoors might be within their means.

The level of advancement within a society will affect the types of recreation as well. Perhaps they don't read books – stories are told orally, memorized and passed down to each generation.

No television? Perhaps there are street-side puppet shows instead!

Forms of Recreation

Games

Games can be a multi-functional form of recreation. While they are entertaining, they also teach skills. Things are always more memorable when they are made to be fun.

Children's Games

Children's games are usually simple, and they are often created on a whim to make a mundane chore more enjoyable. Anything can be made into a contest – who pulls the most weeds, who can find the most eggs (not for Easter, but retrieving from hens), who milked the most cows, etc. Perhaps they were taught to waltz while folding sheets between two people.

Games can also be used to help children use up or channel excess energy, and to teach them manners. Some examples are Red Rover (so dangerous, but so fun), tag, hide 'n seek, the quiet game, and 'Mother May I?'

Adult Games

Games for adults usually require more refined skills than children's games, though not always. The skills developed are often used for more sinister ends, as well.

Games of chance are unpredictable (we're not going to deliberate statistics here) unless one cheats, and usually rely on bluffing skills. Card games (not solitaire), dice games, and betting on odds for sporting events are all games of chance. These types of games also have a higher chance of becoming an addiction.

If a society prizes the ability to do manual labor, strength, or physical fitness, games and recreation will arise out of that. These may be just for fun, or they may have higher stakes, sometimes even being games that are fought to the death.

---

[9] http://phrontistery.info/o.html

Tournaments are a very flexible example of a type of recreation that could happen in any society. It doesn't have to be jousting, but simply pitting several different sets of people against each other multiple times until a sole victor remains. It can be adapted to any type of activity, but is more likely to be games of physical prowess. One example would be the Olympics.

Other types of games or recreation might include wrestling, running, fencing (swords, not property boundaries), or rodeos.

Games that exercise the mind have always been a part of society and culture. They are especially prized among those who make it a habit to think strategically, whether it's plotting the next war, or the next marriage.

Chess is an ancient game, and has been found in many different but similar forms around the world. It is well suited for adaptation to fantasy and science fiction settings.

Riddles are good ways to train your mind to think outside the obvious. Sudoku can teach you about predicting patterns.

Stories

Oral tradition is a fascinating point of study. Often, before written language takes hold, it will be the cornerstone of a community. Sadly, in the transition from oral to written forms, stories are often lost or altered.

Stories can serve a few different purposes.

The most important objective of storytelling, especially oral tradition, is to pass down the history of a group of people. Those responsible for oral history are often trained for years, their memorization checked again and again.

Stories are also used to teach morals. *Aesop's Fables* are some of the more well-known moral tales, and while most of the lessons in those are simple, it's a good starting point for figuring out little proverbs that might be shared in your world.

Also consider how current events might influence children's stories. Many nursery rhymes were actually political commentary when they were written, such as 'Humpty-Dumpty' and 'Jack and Jill.'

And of course, there are stories that exist just for enjoyment. History and morality may still be entwined in them, but sometimes the harshness of life simply demands an escape. These stories are often hopeful – the good guys always win, there's always enough food for everyone, and no one dies.

Celebrations

Celebrations accomplish two things: they improve the morale of the community, and they help people bond with each other. That bond is important in times of crises, whether that be famine, drought, plague, or war, just to name a few.

How connected one feels to their community will make a difference in how they react to catastrophe. Do they join together and work as a team with their community, or do they take off on their own, each to fend for themselves?

There are many different kinds of celebrations that might be incorporated into your stories.

Personal celebrations will be events like birthdays, betrothals, marriages, etc. Many of these may be communally celebrated, but they are personal in *origin*, and they can happen at any time.

Seasonal celebrations happen around the same time each year, but aren't connected to any other major events. These might be celebrations at the time of the first spring planting, when the crops are all harvested, or at the solstices and equinoxes. There may be additional celebrations as well, when a resource becomes available again – like the first time each year when the lake has frozen over solidly enough to finally skate, or when the maple sap runs (and can be tapped for maple syrup!) right at the cusp of springtime.

Religious celebrations are often of a memorial nature – whether of an event, a death, or even a resurrection – but can be personal as well, such as a christening, baptism, or wedding. These may eventually turn into culturally recognized holidays, sometimes following a seasonal pattern – such as Christmas.

Civil celebrations are a celebration of the people who make up society, or commemorations of events that benefited them, at least at first. In the United States, these are holidays like Independence Day or Labor Day. There may also be commemorations of discoveries – scientific breakthroughs, new land masses, etc.

Memorial celebrations can be related to religious celebrations, but not always. These often take a more somber feel, at least for a while, until people forget what the memorial was actually for. These types of celebrations will often be commemorative of a battle, the death of a beloved monarch, or the mass death of part of the population (perhaps from plague or an unexpected natural disaster).

Other Forms of Recreation

There are so many forms of recreation that we couldn't possibly go over all of them. Don't forget about hobbies – anything can be a hobby, though many of the things we call hobbies in first world society are things our ancestors, and those in developing nations, had to do for survival.

And, of course, there's always the thing that happens when people are snowed in, or rained in, or just plain old bored and have too much time on their hands - sex.

Other Inspiration

A culture's recreation and forms of entertainment often become a defining part of their society and history. Look at ways you can work certain aspects of that into the reputation of the societies you are creating. Stereotypes will appear from there, and while you certainly shouldn't stereotype your own story, your characters *will* stereotype each other. Have fun with it!

'Oblectation' Exercises

1. What are one or two simple children's games everyone knows?

Examples: hopscotch, jump rope, hide 'n seek.

2. What is a more dangerous children's game that while it isn't deadly, still sometimes ends in injury?

Like Red Rover, King of the Hill, or daring each other to do stupid things.

3. What are a few games adults enjoy?

List at least one game of chance, one game that shows off physical prowess, and one logic or puzzle game.

4. What are some activities that would be enjoyed by the community as a whole with participants of all ages?

Sporting events, neighborhood parties, a traveling circus, etc.

5. How are stories shared in your world?

Do they have a way to write things down yet, or is it still oral? If oral, is it spoken, or perhaps sung? What about 'sharing' memories directly between people, like a mind-meld?

_____

_____

_____

_____

_____

_____

_____

_____

6. What is the most well-known story?

Something everyone knows – it is likely to be a creation story, a warning, some sort of propaganda to create loyalty to monarch, or a set of values. It might be portrayed as good vs. evil or us against them.

_____

_____

_____

_____

_____

_____

_____

_____

The A-Zs of Worldbuilding

7. What are some common historical stories that are passed around, and how does the same story change depending on who's telling it?

Everything has a different point of view.

8. What are some ideas for short, moral stories?

These will often be stories that can be condensed into an example or proverb.

9. What are a couple just-for-fun stories?
Something to make people laugh or smile.

10. What is one major celebration of each type (seasonal, religious, civil, memorial) that are celebrated by your culture?
You don't have to elaborate on it very much right now, just what and why.

The A-Zs of Worldbuilding

11. What personal events are celebrated?

Are birthdays celebrated, or is it just another day? What about coming of age, betrothals/engagements, job offers, etc.?

12. What hobbies are common?

These may still be useful, but something a person prefers to do over another thing. Like crocheting vs. knitting.

13. What resources are you using for creating oblectation for your world?

P is for Plants
The Beauty and Function of Nature

Plants are something we interact with almost daily – unless you don't leave your house, of course, and assuming you don't have any potted plants.

We rely on plants for food production, for medicine, and for simple enjoyment. There's wonderfully unique beauty in a field full of blooming wildflowers, or a patch of clover filled with the buzzing busy-ness of honeybees, or the quiet, innocuous scattering of violets that like to hide where you least expect them.

Knowing which plants like certain kinds of soil can help someone plant a bountiful garden. Certain plants can help identify the pH of nearby water sources. Knowing which plants have very deep root systems can be helpful for finding underground water sources, too, and just how deep it might be.

While neither your characters – nor you – need to be adept at 'reading plants,' you should have at least a few basics figured out.

Food

Grains, vegetables, fruits, nuts, and fungi (like mushrooms) are all food sources. They can be cultivated and bred for more desirable traits, though some of them will always grow better 'wild' and be tastier when foraged.

There's no limit on what you can do with these types of plants. Grains are multi-purpose. They can be ground into flour to make bread, sprouted and grown for a few days to turn into greens, or used for brewing alcohol. Root vegetables are quite versatile as well. There are many root varieties that grow in different climates (though they all store best in cool temperatures). Root vegetables and grains all have one thing in common: they are starchy.

***Herbs** are plants where the leaves and stems can be used either fresh or dried for adding flavor to food. They often have medicinal qualities as well. Occasionally, the root is used as well.*

***Spices** are plants which are typically dried and ground up before use, but not always. They are more likely to be derived from the seeds, roots, and bark of plants. Spices have a stronger, more pungent flavor than herbs.*

Some plants do double-duty and appear in the kitchen as both herbs and spices. Cilantro (more often known as coriander outside the United States) is used both for its leaves as a fresh herb, and its seed for a spice. Sometimes the same fruit of a plant is used for two different spices. The nutmeg grows on a tree – it is actually the seed – encased in a shell. Inside the shell, the nutmeg itself is wrapped in the *aril*, which you may know of as the spice *mace*.

The food some plants produce will be considered a delicacy. There are many factors at play in this: the growing conditions required, how long the produce would be in season (a shorter season means more limited supply), how long the item lasts (berries spoil quickly, peaches easily bruise, but apples will last months in the right conditions), and how difficult it is to harvest (if you're curious for an example, just look up what exactly saffron is and how it's harvested).

Medicine

Most herbs and spices have medicinal qualities as well as culinary ones. Some are also poisonous in large of doses/servings, as well. Some aren't poisonous unless you mix them very specifically. Take that for your plot as you will!

Even if your society is more advanced and has medical facilities and pharmaceuticals, state-of-the-art surgery theaters and x-rays, somewhere in your world where they can't afford or access those things, there is probably a 'wise one' who knows how to cure almost anything with plants.

A well-known medicinal herb in speculative fiction history might be *athelas* (or *Kingsfoil*) from *The Lord of the Rings*.

Kingsfoil was the common name for *athelas* (this was its Elvish name), and in the peaceful Shire there was no need of its medicinal properties, so the Hobbits simply knew of it as a weed and literally fed it to their pigs. Those must have been some really healthy pigs.

Almost everywhere else in Middle-earth, though, whether it was called *Kingsfoil* or *athelas*, they knew how to use it to draw poison out of wounds. And it was incredibly simple – all that needed to be done was to crush it, and apply it to the wound.

Since the medicinal uses for plants are often discovered accidentally, keep in mind that just because a plant may be found in multiple regions doesn't mean that everyone uses it the same way and for the same things.

Beauty

Each season has a beauty of its own.

Spring will be full of fresh, green leaves. There are lots of flowers, especially on the plants and trees that are going to set fruit.

Summer will see mature plants and growing fruit, as it prepares to finish growing. Harvest actually starts in the summer, and with a few exceptions, is well finished by the time autumn arrives.

Autumn will bring colors from falling leaves, and hues of brown will begin to make themselves known with accents of red and yellow and orange, and sometimes even purple.

Winter will bring bleak landscapes of brown and gray and white, with pops of color here and there. Evergreen plants will give random green accents, and often there will be berries that are still clinging to shrubs through the winter.

The colors of nature may be completely different in your fictional world, but they will still follow the pattern of seasons unless you have a steady (near an equator) or extreme (near poles or *on* the equator) climate. Spring will be bright and vivid, summer will be steady, but start slowly fading in the last month or so. Autumn will have a last splash of color against a dark background, and winter will be muted tones.

Region & Climate

Different plants are suited for different areas and growth conditions. Plants growing near a coastline will need to have a high tolerance for the salt levels that will be found in the soil there. Mountains tend to be rocky, so root vegetables will be a challenge to grow in those locations even when the soil is loose, simply because there will be more debris in it. Nearly everything likes to grow near rivers, because there is plenty of water. Succulents are the exception. However, it is possible to overwater just about any type of vegetation. Everything has a limit on how much water it can absorb, and it will cause things to split open (fruit bearing plants especially) or drown (plants need oxygen and nutrients at their root system as much as they need water).

In polar climates, inhabitants will face the challenge of very short growing seasons, but there may be extended daylight in the summer (think of the midnight sun seen in places like Alaska and Norway, anywhere very far north) to help with vegetation growth. Plants really only need a few things to thrive – water, nutrients, and light. But if you create plants that don't use photosynthesis to convert nutrients, then you'll be looking at vegetation that may die from light.

Temperature is another important factor. There are very few plants on Earth that thrive in below-freezing temperatures, but in general plants are more forgiving and tolerant than we expect of them. Certain plants will still grow even in temperatures too hot or too cold for their preference, but there will be unintended side effects – like cabbage and lettuce will become bitter in hot weather, and it will 'bolt' to produce seed. Temperature extremes in both directions can cause plants to go dormant until conditions are more favorable for them.

Don't forget to consider how your plants propagate. Look up terms like *open, self,* and *cross pollination*. Plants can also be hybrids, or propagated by cuttings of stems, leaves, or roots.

Other Inspiration

The best inspiration you can find for plants is to go outside and look at them. Find a local farm that does tours, especially a pick-your-own place where you can get up close and personal with the plants.

Look through gardening and botany books, and if you're wanting to use non-conventional medicines in your world/stories, look up some herbalism sources (The Herbal Academy, Chestnut School of Herbal Medicine, and Mountain Rose Herbs all have excellent blogs and many other free resources). Consider putting together a *materia medica*[10] for your world if it's going to play an extensive role.

Don't be afraid to use the same plants that we have, especially if you're creating an earth-like setting. There so many different, bizarre things in our world that you can just tweak a little bit. Don't forget about carnivorous plants!

---

[10] *Materia medica* is a Latin term that means 'medical material.' In modern times, it is usually a collection of medical treatments and remedies that has been put together by someone for their own reference.

P is for Plants

'Plants' Exercises

1. What are your main sources of grain?

Do they grind anything for flour, or cook the grains whole and eat them like cereal? What are they called? Give at least two examples.

_____
_____
_____
_____
_____
_____
_____
_____
_____

2. What are the two most popular vegetables? The one most hated?

Potatoes, beets, carrots, green beans... some people love them, some people hate them! Broccoli has a reputation for being disliked.

_____
_____
_____
_____
_____
_____
_____
_____
_____

The A-Zs of Worldbuilding

3. What are the most popular fruits?

Apples, strawberries, melons. Something can be popular because it's easy to preserve, too, even if it's not extremely tasty.

4. Are there any fruits or vegetables that 'masquerade' as a member of the other group?

Tomatoes are considered to technically be a fruit, but are used as a vegetable most of the time.

P is for Plants

5. What are three herbs you'll find in any kitchen in your world, and what plants do they come from (if their names differ)?

Parsley is probably one of the most well-known herbs. It goes with just about everything.

6. What are three spices you'll find in any kitchen, and what plants do they come from (if their names differ)?

Like black pepper, or cinnamon. But not salt, because salt, while used as a spice/seasoning, is a mineral.

143

The A-Zs of Worldbuilding

7. What plants (and their fruit) are considered a delicacy?

Artichokes take a lot of space with relatively small yield, for example. Or saffron, which requires a large amount of labor for just a small amount of spice. Orchids are an exotic decorative flower, except in their native habitat where they grow wild.

_____
_____
_____
_____
_____
_____
_____
_____
_____
_____

8. From the herbs you listed previously, choose at least two that have medicinal properties and explain how they are used.

Parsley and rosemary, for example, are both antibacterial, among other things. Are these varieties commonly known throughout your world?

_____
_____
_____
_____
_____
_____
_____
_____
_____
_____

9. From the spices you listed previously, choose at least two that have medicinal properties and explain how they are used.

Ginger helps soothe muscle aches. Turmeric is thought to help chronic pain, for example, though most spices must be taken in far greater amounts than they are used in flavoring dishes to get their full medicinal side effects.

10. Name 2-3 more herbs, spices, or flowers that are used for medicinal purposes but not commonly used (if used at all) for culinary purposes, and explain how they are used.

A certain variety of the hibiscus flower can be used to lower blood pressure, for example. Chamomile is another one we're familiar with, often used for insomnia, relaxation, or to treat headaches.

The A-Zs of Worldbuilding

11. What plants might be used for recreational purposes?

Things like tobacco and other... more questionably legal plants.

12. Are there any plants that are reserved for special use, or considered taboo?

Maybe a plant is only allowed to be used for incense by religious leaders, for example. For taboo plants, these might also be some of the recreational ones you've decided on above, because addiction is always an ugly thing.

13. Out of all the plants you've created, which ones are subject to the most stringent growing requirements?

These will be the rarest plants, but will have a peak period of abundance – whether that is once a year, or even every few years, depending on the plant's life cycle.

14. What are some common flowers that are seen in your world, but are mainly only appreciated for their beauty? What do they look like?

Many of these may be edible or medicinal as well, but aren't commonly recognized for those properties. More people know of roses and enjoy their look than know that they can be used in cooking.

15. What resources are you using for creating your plant life in your world?

P is for Plants

Q is for Queens
The Role of Fictional Governments

Many fantasy writers deal with monarchies as their government of choice. A lot of science fiction veers toward a totalitarian government, or a (sometimes pseudo-) democratic government, depending on whether or not it is dystopian fiction. (Disclaimer: I have not read a ton of sci-fi, so don't take this completely at my own word. It's just what I've observed in the sci-fi I have read or watched.)

As a general rule, when a government is first founded, it is established for the benefit of its citizens. Occasionally, a government is founded (or overthrown) simply in the pursuit of power by an individual or a group.

It is rare for there to be a gathering of people – let alone an established country – that has no infrastructure for authority and power. Most people want a leader to take care of things, and there is usually someone willing to step up for the position, whether their intentions are honorable or not.

Types of Government

No Established Government

For small groups of people, this is certainly an option, though any form of council will still have the feel of certain types of government depending on how it is run.

There is also the option of anarchy (each person for themselves), if it plays into the role you need for your story.

Monarchy

One person or family holds the power. There are *absolute* monarchies and *limited* monarchies (where there is a secondary branch of government that balances the reach of the ruler), but the monarchy itself is usually passed down through heirs.

Oligarchy

A few people hold power, usually a group of people with some sort of privilege, whether that be influence, wealth, land ownership, etc.

Theocracy

The head of the government, usually a monarch (but not always), is a divine being, or also the head of the state religion. The government's main purpose is furthering the interests of that specific deity or religion.

Plutocracy

The government consists of the wealthy. Money equals power.

Republic

A government that has elected representatives chosen by its citizens, and *does not* have a head of state who inherits that position by birthright.

Democracy

A government where power is exercised by the people, usually through votes, and the majority rules. They may or may not have elected representatives.

There are many more types of government. Don't hesitate to hunt something else down if none of these work for your story.

Government and Your Plot

Speculative fiction often has political undertones (or overtones). The political intricacies can often be invisible in the midst of war, though, and even in the history of that war later. Much happens behind the closed doors of those in power.

That is not an excuse for you, as the author, to not know what is happening behind those closed doors, though. Even beyond worldbuilding, there will always be things you don't include in your story that are still vital to the plot.

Government is a powerful plot tool, but it can be complicated, so establish your ground rules ahead of time. Nothing sucks more than realizing the government is involved in a situation with the plot, and you have to stop everything to figure out exactly *how* they're involved and what their authority is.

Even knowing something as simple as what type of government runs the place can save you a lot of trouble.

Other Inspiration

Types of government can be hybridized. The United States is supposed to be a Constitutional republic, though it's more like a plutocracy or oligarchy these days.

England is a great example of a limited monarchy, combined with parliamentary representation.

There are, of course, several things I didn't touch on here – Communism, Socialism, Fascism, etc. They all have parts where they are functional, and where they just aren't.

Whenever there is an oppressive government in power, don't forget to look for where underground movements exist. They will *always* exist. It may be religious (look up the underground church movements in long-established Communist countries, for example), it may be cultural or economic (black markets to buy/sell/trade things that may have once been commonly found but are now forbidden – as well as legitimately illegal items, such as human trafficking), it may be spy networks, or ways to get people what they need to survive. Don't forget the existence of smugglers – some may actually be doing illegal business, but some may be breaking the law for ethical reasons.

'Queens' Exercises

1. Is there an established government? Is it local, national, global, intergalactic? What type of structure does it have?

For example, a king would be the head of a monarchy that governed a nation – no matter what size the nation might be. A mayor would govern a smaller region, usually only a single town. Types of structure are monarchy, democracy, communist, socialist, oligarchy, etc.

___

2. If not, is the society in a state of anarchy? Or are there small, local governments?

These small local governments can be a council, a specific family, a group of elders... even a mayor.

3. How long has the government been established, and how was it established?

There are numerous ways this can happen – divine appointment, election of the people, someone simply stepping into the leadership position when no one else will. The how *of governance is often based in the culture.*

_____
_____
_____
_____
_____
_____
_____
_____
_____
_____

4. How much power do they have – whether power given by the citizens, or taken by force – to affect daily life?

What is the government allowed to do? What is it not allowed to do?

_____
_____
_____
_____
_____
_____
_____
_____

The A-Zs of Worldbuilding

5. Does the government concern itself with nuances, or just with making sure the important things happen? What do they deem to be important or non-important?

What does the government actually care to do? Are they in charge of infrastructure, defense, maintaining a money standard? What about foreign relations? How important is it that they exert total control?

\
\
\
\
\
\
\
\
\
\

6. Who benefits the most from the current form of government?

These will be the most ardent supporters, whether they are right or wrong.

7. Who benefits the least?

These will be viewed as rebels, whether their reasons are just or not. Is this underclass status permanent, or can one's status be elevated? How would that happen? Examples might be knighthood, starting a successful business (thereby increasing wealth), or even buying a citizenship rank.

8. What would happen if the leader of the government was assassinated?

What would be the social and political ramifications? Who would feel it the most?

9. What resources are you using for creating your governments?

Q is for Queens

R is for Religion
When Belief is More Than Superstition

I could write an entire book on this topic alone. Religion is an intricate subject, whether you're tackling it in fiction or in real life[11].

You are not going to need to know all the answers to *all* of the questions addressed in this chapter if religion doesn't play a major role in your story. However, if religion is an important aspect for even one of your *characters*, you should read through this and make note of anything that might affect how that character lives.

At the least, be aware that there are religions present in your world, and they will interact with each other and society, and know how they might do so. Most of your characters will not know the entire history of their religion and/or culture. There will be many things they simply do because it was what they were *taught* to do.

Why is Religion Important?

Unless you're dealing with characters, peoples, and civilizations vastly different from humanity (and if this is the case, will your readers be able to relate to them?) it will be nearly impossible for religion not to exist.

Cultures and religions are deeply entwined together. Judaism, Islam, and Hinduism are both three well-known examples of how religion affects a culture, and can become nearly inseparable from it. Numerous more examples exist.

When someone is sincere in their beliefs, no matter what the religion is, it affects an infinite number of things. It changes the way a person thinks about the past, the present, and the future. It changes how they react to circumstances, and it changes how they react to the thought and reality of death.

Being religious or not is a deeply personal experience, and no matter where your characters fall on the religion spectrum, you must understand why they make the choices they do.

Creating a religion for a speculative fiction setting has a comforting certainty to it, though. You get to decide what is truth and what is not. And even if you know, don't discount the power of leaving it ambiguous for your characters or your readers.

Keep in mind that time can make truth become myth, though, especially as eyewitnesses to an event die off. And even if you have inhabitants in your world who are immortal, as more generations are born who have not witnessed a (or *the*) mythical event, they may begin to disbelieve simply because it becomes a divine truth by 'hearsay' only.

Cults & Religion

For clarity's sake, any references in this chapter to cults are going to follow the modern definition that most people are familiar with: a religion that is extremist or unorthodox (often but not always having split away from a more established, traditional religion) in nature.

---

[11] In 2014, I wrote a series of articles on worldbuilding religion for Fantasy-Faction.com. Some of the content of this chapter was first seen in these posts. You can find them here for comparison:
http://fantasy-faction.com/2014/worldbuilding-a-religion-part-one-religion-vs-cult
http://fantasy-faction.com/2014/worldbuilding-a-religion-part-two-creating-religion-and-culture
http://fantasy-faction.com/2014/worldbuilding-a-religion-part-three-how-religion-shapes-characters

The characteristics of cults and religions are very similar, but it's mainly how the leaders handle power and authority that separates the two from each other. Religious leaders (unless the power has gone to their heads) usually go to the effort to remain accountable to their own leaders, peers, and followers. Cult leaders have a specific agenda they are trying to fulfill, and sometimes they wholly believe the message they are espousing (or they are insane) and other times it's all a big con.

Any religion can become a cult, when leadership (either of a local sect, or of the entire religion) grows out of control. Conversely, a cult can become an established religion, especially over time as beliefs may mellow, and the original leaders die off.

Don't discount the plot usage you can get out of a cult. Just don't make *all* your religions cult-like.

Before Organized Religion

Belief and faith exist even outside of organized religion. Depending on the era your story is set in for your world, organized religions may not yet be established.

Consider what your inhabitants believe in the early days of their societies. There are numerous ways these beliefs might evolve, including interaction with a spiritual being or realm, reverence for nature and how it supplies for their needs, unexplained natural phenomena, and fear (especially fear of death).

The absence or existence of suffering will also influence the beliefs of your inhabitants, either to explain why it exists (good vs. evil, for example) or to explain why it doesn't.

Establishing Religion

You don't have to know everything about why your characters believe what they do right away. A good start to developing a religion is to look at what your characters (and their culture/society) value, and then define it in a theme.

Let's say that you want to develop a religion that sees nature as sacred. Write that down, and then look at where your inhabitants are and start asking *why* questions.

Why might a culture revere nature? It could be because they see that nature provides for them in abundance, or perhaps nature and all its resources is withering away and they worship it because they long for it to return.

If nature is sacred, what does that mean for their way of life? Is permission required for using certain resources? Are any resources strictly prohibited? Do any of the permissions or restrictions seem out of place for the culture, or do they all make sense?

If, for example, they are prohibited to cut down trees for lumber, then it could easily morph into being forbidden to use wood at all, especially a few hundred years down the road when the original instructions might have been distorted.

Belief Systems

There are many options for your world here – monotheism (one god), polytheism (many gods), animism (everything has a soul – including inanimate objects), reincarnation (a soul returns as a different person/creature again and again until it reaches perfection), etc. If you haven't already determined the existence or reality of an afterlife (see D is for Death), do take some time to do so now. Either way, figure out how the afterlife, or lack of it, works with the belief systems for your cultures.

The A-Zs of Worldbuilding

Belief systems can easily be mashed together by your cultures, especially as inhabitants migrate and merge with other groups.

Rituals and worship will evolve out of a specific belief system as well. In a culture with a polytheistic faith, someone who chooses to worship only one of those gods may be seen as an anomaly, especially if worship of *all* the gods is implicit to the culture. Animism may require that permission is asked (and/or granted) before one does certain things, like sitting in a chair, cutting down a tree, or slaughtering your chicken for dinner.

As you develop rituals and/or worship ceremonies for your religions, keep in mind that they serve two purposes: bringing people together under one uniting front (sometimes to the deliberate exclusion of others), and also to make belief *personal*. Rituals especially are ways to help a person to remember specific things.

Religion, Culture, and Society – Cooperation & Clash

Dominant religions (the beliefs held by a majority of citizens) will affect a culture as it develops. A cultural religion (one everyone adheres to, at least in public) can also have a cult-like feel to it without being an actual cult. Even when someone disagrees with the public beliefs, they may simply not speak up about it or not openly practice another religion because they don't want to be publicly ostracized.

The morals that a faith espouses may become the groundwork of the legal laws of a country. The rituals of a belief system will also affect the day-to-day life of people within a society, and some of those rituals may become so ingrained in a culture that even those outside a belief system still perform them. An example would be such as when people say, "Bless you!" when someone sneezes, because at one time people believed that your soul left your body when you sneezed. 'God bless you!' was the incantation, essentially, to get your soul back where it belonged – inside your body – before you were possessed by something else. It has been shortened, over time, to just, 'Bless you!'

Religion can also be used to ensure the survival of a culture by being integrated into the day-to-day life of a community. Rituals and traditions to mark certain waypoints of a child's life are one way of doing this, because they are often seen as a communal event. Several examples of this from our world would be events like baptisms, circumcision, Confirmation and First Communion, and bar and bat mitzvahs[12].

The ways religion can be integrated into memorable occasions are countless. First, look at what you've established with your religion so far, and then see how the main tenets and mythology can be made symbolic for everyday life.

Some religions will also dictate manners of dress, acceptable lifestyles (including sexuality), or holidays. The more complicated the rules of a religion are, and especially if they are mandated by the ruling authorities, the more oppressed your characters may seem to be, even if that's not what you intended for your story. There can be a lot of rules if you want, but it's one of those matters where you need to decide how much you share with your readers. It all depends on what you want to accomplish with your story.

When there is only one (or only a few) dominant religions within a society, society at large will likely hold religious adherents to different standards than non-religious (or religion-unknown) citizens. Those standards may be higher or lower, depending on how the religion is viewed by outsiders, as well as how loudly religious morals may be broadcast.

---

[12] You may also wish to refer to the chapters B is for Birth (pg. 12) and Y is for Youth (pg. 228).

If a religion makes a point of doing charitable works, being honest to a fault, treating all people equally, etc., people outside of that religion will be looking to see if those who follow it actually live up to its standards. For those within the religion, it can put pressure on them to be more than they are capable of, and a balance has to be found. Unrealistic pressure can cause someone to take drastic actions, though, and this is where you can start finding story fodder!

Religion and Your Characters

One important thing to keep in mind as you create your characters and worldbuild your religions is what your character's first encounter with religion was like. That first encounter, and whether it was negative or positive, is what will set up their expectations for religion in the future.

Positive first encounters do not guarantee life-long devotion, though. Particularly for characters who might have first been exposed to a cult (either of their own choice, or by being dragged into it by a guardian), where you're drawn in with promises and have suddenly found you've bitten off more than you can chew. A negative first impression may also be tempered if your character knows that the person giving the example holds no sway within a religious sect.

For many characters, a first exposure to religion will be through their family. It's one thing to observe those who practice a religion from outside of their lives, in limited exposure. It's completely different to observe it up close and personal, and to see every flaw, failing, and hypocrisy.

Even when a character's family doesn't adhere to a specific religion (or any religion at all) their behavior will influence how your character treats religion themselves. Sometimes that means they mimic the behavior they have witnessed, or something may cause them to veer in the opposite direction, no matter whether they were brought up in a specific religion and respectful of it, or if they were taught that all religion is a sham.

Ultimately, what your character believes and why they believe it will be deeply personal to them. Knowing these things, as the writer, can aid you in developing their personality and understanding how and why they react to certain things. Faith in a higher power can be both a source of fear (eternal damnation, for instance) and a source of strength (knowing that somehow, despite circumstances, is going to be okay in the end even if they themselves feel powerless).

Other Inspiration

Religion brings people together in many ways, but it can also be extremely divisive. Everything that makes a religion unique and attracts people to it can also be used to persecute it.

Fantasy worlds and fantasy religions should not be black and white. They reflect our own worlds and our inner thoughts, even unintentionally. This is what gives them depth, and helps make the stories connect with our readers, so don't be afraid to get your hands a little dirty.

When you're looking for complexity in your religion worldbuilding, just look around you and see what you can tweak from your own experiences, or from what friends and family have experienced. Even if someone adheres to a faith that is not a minority religion, bullies still exist everywhere – even within a religion – and at some point, everyone who believes something has been mocked for it.

Don't blindly pick and choose which religious elements you use from the real world, though. There are many personal and cultural nuances to having faith in something, and if you aren't careful in how you use an element it's easy to fall into the habit of perpetuating stereotypes. Be creative, *because* religion can be very inflammatory subject when handled poorly. This doesn't mean that all your fictional religions must be positive, but be careful about the underlying connotations you may be find yourself writing about *real* religions.

The key to believability – in all your worldbuilding, not just religions – is creating something that resonates with what your readers already know, while showing them something new and wonderful along the way.

'Religion' Exercises

1. If (when) there is no organized religion, what spiritual beliefs exist in your world?

Is there one all-powerful being that is worshipped (and likely viewed as the creator) or are there many such beings? Do they believe in the existence of spirits, or only what can be seen?

_____

2. How do their beliefs about death affect their beliefs in life?

Refer back to the D is for Death chapter & exercises (pg. 28). If they do not believe in an afterlife, or that one can know if there is an afterlife before reaching it, there may be some fear and 'live in the moment' mentality. It may also make killing and murder a more serious offense, since that would be making someone no longer exist. For those who do believe in an afterlife, do ancestral spirits play a role at all? Even in religions that do not have ancestor worship, there is often still the belief that those who have died before are still watching over their loved ones.

3. How do your inhabitants balance their beliefs with the existence of suffering?

What does good vs. evil look like in your world? How much of a role does free will play, and how does that interact with spiritual beliefs, especially if there is a god or gods.

_____
_____
_____
_____
_____
_____
_____
_____

4. What brought about the change from non-organized spiritual beliefs into organized religion in your world?

It might be something as simple as bringing a community closer together, or as complex as a divine intervention and revelation.

_____
_____
_____
_____
_____
_____
_____
_____

5. Is your fictional religion based on truth, myth, or a combination of both?
Did it begin with an actual event or person? Or was it simply made up by someone to fulfill a role?

_____

6. Who/what began the religion?
A divine entity, or a person seeking something?

The A-Zs of Worldbuilding

7. How is the religion organized? Is it commonly known with a large amount of followers, or small and still in its beginning stages?

Are there multiple leaders? Is the leadership well-balanced, or do they have ulterior motives? Is there anything questionable about how people are convinced to convert?

_____

8. What is the purpose of the religion?

Does it exist to help people co-exist peacefully? To spread a divine truth? To offer escape from death?

_____

9. If there was one rule to concisely portray the core belief of your religion, what would it be?
Think of something like the Golden Rule (do unto others...).

_____

_____

_____

_____

_____

_____

_____

_____

_____

10. What are the major tenets of each religion?
These are their core beliefs – the foundations that make each religion unique.

_____

_____

_____

_____

_____

_____

_____

_____

_____

11. What is the one core belief (creed) that cannot be compromised if one wishes to still call themselves a follower of a specific religion?

Examples from our world would be the Nicene Creed (Christianity – and there are many variations of this creed that have been adapted over time, but the Nicene is the one that could be considered the original), the Sh'ma Yisrael (Judaism), and the Shahada (Islam).

12. What incentive does the religion offer to bring in followers?

Riches, eternal life, true love? Protecting against evil? A home? This will usually tie in with the purpose of the religion, but not always.

13. What does each religion demand of its followers?

What are they required to do? Give up their riches? Swear loyalty to a certain deity? Slaughter their firstborn (or, less gruesome, set them aside for religious service, such as a priesthood)?

14. Are there rituals or sacrifices required?

How do worshipers show their devotion in day-to-day life, or on religious holidays?

The A-Zs of Worldbuilding

15. How does each religion view potentially controversial issues such as the use of magic, prophecy, divination, etc.?

What is permitted to the followers of each religion, and what is not? Go a step further and figure out why something is permitted or prohibited, as well, not just that is simply is. Some reasons might be that it is dangerous (perhaps people have died because they can't control magic) or because it is seen as distracting (either from day-to-day life, or from furthering religious practice).

16. Who are the major players within a religion?

The hierarchy of power, any saints, something that is considered the 'enemy' (EG: Satan).

17. What religions are so old no one remembers how they began?
Superstitions usually arise from these kinds of religions. A talisman or charm may be used because someone saw their grandmother do so, without knowing the meaning behind it. If you're worldbuilding a young world, you can skip this question.

_____

18. What religions are new?
'New' is a relative term, but usually refers to a religion currently being formed, or where people are still living who witnessed its birth.

19. What is the greatest good each religion has done in your world?
Perhaps a major plague was stopped through a miracle, or a war. Perhaps poverty was abolished.

20. What is the greatest evil each religion has done in your world?
The road to hell is paved with good intentions, after all.

21. How do these religions clash with each other?

Why aren't they all just one religion? What makes them irreconcilable?

22. What do they all agree on?

Caring for the poor and respect for the elders is something found in nearly every religion in our world, for example.

The A-Zs of Worldbuilding

23. What lifetime milestones is religion highly involved in?

Birth, coming of age, marriage, grief, death, just to name some of them. What kinds of rituals are associated with these occasions?

___

24. How does the local economy make a profit from religion?

Selling talismans, idols, blessings/curses/spells, sacrifices that meet certain criteria, etc. Catering to pilgrims traveling to significant religious sites will also be a major economic boon.

25. How much control does the local, prominent religion have over social matters?
Does it have any say on public policy?

26. What was the first instance of religious persecution for the culture you're worldbuilding now?
Persecution will happen, even if there is a state-mandated religion that everyone follows. There will be differences in beliefs between sects, and infighting can be as much a source of persecution as government control can.

The A-Zs of Worldbuilding

27. Have there been any religious martyrs?
Martyrs are those who die for their beliefs, rather than give them up.

28. Who are some iconic persons from the religion you're creating?
This could be the founder of the faith, those who are saints or evolving deities, incarnate deities, or people who were influential in a reformation of a faith, and martyrs nominated for/granted sainthood, etc.

29. What resources are you using from our world for creating your religions?

S is for Science
When the Story Demands 'How'

The pursuit of knowledge is a never-ending quest, and it leads to the development of medicine, technology, and other scientific fields. It may sometimes be a forbidden path (perhaps justly so – like human transmutation in Fullmetal Alchemist), or a bloody one.

Different societies and cultures will prioritize different things. Not all branches of science will exist in different worlds, nor will they advance at the same rate.

Science is a massive undertaking, both in real life and in fiction. You may need to know more about science depending on what you're writing (especially if you're writing hard science fiction), but remember that your goal is, ultimately, to tell a good story.

The Priority of Science

Whether or not your people pursue science will depend on a few factors: how much time they have to pursue anything beyond their survival, how many supplies and tools they have access to, and censorship.

People who have to work every day in the fields, or making wares to sell, will usually not have the leisure time to spend pursuing the why of things that don't guarantee their day-to-day survival.

Likewise, those ensuring their survival usually do not have the extra funds to devote to the specialized equipment often required for scientific research or experiments. Time can always be found, though, even at the detriment of other priorities. And sometimes sheer determination can see someone through to a certain point, but they will hit a wall eventually.

Censorship does not always have to be done by the government. Concerned parents may restrict access to materials they think are foolish for a curious youngster, a religious organization may have to approve all reading materials, or another researcher or scientist may be closely guarding any materials they have access to.

How the World Works

To some extent, even if it's not considered *formal* science, anything that works with observation and testing of how things function and reproduce is science.

Even without being aware of it, anyone who grows food will practice agricultural science if they simply pay attention to how types of plants breed (or cross-breed), what types of soil the plants like, and how much water they need to thrive.

Baking is a form of science – whether growing sourdough starter for the next batch of bread, or figuring out how much baking powder or yeast needs to go in a dish to get the correct amount of bubbling in the dough.

Science vs. Magic

Magic and science are not always at odds, though they can be.

There are several ways to approach this topic. Look at our own history, for example. Even some of the most advanced scientists from as little as two hundred years ago would be shocked at the advances in our world today, and some of them *would* seem downright magical.

Magic can work very, very similarly to science. Often people think that magic is a way to make anything happen easily, but a good writer recognizes what *stakes* can add to a story. Don't make magic the easy way out of a situation. Make it cost something.

Just like science doesn't just *do* what we want it to. It has a set of rules that it works within.

Magic Systems

It's easy to just sit down and say, "Well, my characters can do XYZ because *magic.*" and use it as an excuse for making anything or everything possible. But when you make *everything* possible, you lose a very real function of storytelling: stakes.

A story falls apart if there are no stakes. No stakes means there is nothing pushing your character to learn and grow, and there's no reason for your readers to keep turning the pages.

But making what *seems* impossible *become* possible is exactly what magic is about – not making *anything* possible at no cost.

Magic can be very similar to science, and also have far more variations in practice and rules. The main thing to remember is that you must follow your own established rules for magic within each story, just like science has laws that it works within. However, while science has the same laws that apply fairly universally to all fields, magic can have different rules for each discipline.

The guidelines you will need to apply for magic systems are going to be the **cost** of magic, **who can use** magic and *why* they can, and the **limitations** of magic. All of these can easily be tied into the types of magic that you might want to incorporate into a story.

Elemental magic (air, earth, water, some people include fire and/or spirit, etc.) with those guidelines might look something like this:

Element: Air
Who can use it: Those born outdoors on the night of the full moon.
Cost: The breath in their lungs – amount required may vary by the type of task. Tugging at someone's hair with the wind may be a small task that only requires a puff of breath, but causing a windstorm may require all the air in someone's lungs.
Limitations: Air magic can only be used by practitioners in places where they have physically visited.

That is a very rough, simple system, but it's an example of how you can take an idea, lay down the groundwork, and then expand as you need to while you write. The possibilities are endless, it simply depends on what you need a specific type of magic to do. With the air magic mentioned above, someone may be able to do more than just control wind. If they can control oxygen, then they could also extinguish fires and make toxic air breathable, or safe air unbreathable, etc.

There are many other types of magic that you can use and create for your stories. White or black magic (typically portrayed as good vs. evil, but can be handled in different ways as well), blood magic (often based on the use of one's life force), necromancy (death magic), and many other variations exist or are just waiting for you to create them for your story!

Other Inspiration

There is a lot of wonder – whether magical or scientific – that surrounds us already, and it's waiting for us to just notice it. Pursue the things that interest you, and often a story will follow. And don't feel that you have to reinvent the wheel, or DNA, for your story unless it's absolutely vital to your plot.

'Science' Exercises

1. Is there any pursuit of scientific knowledge? Why or why not?

Is the study of science formalized, or can anyone do it? What might prohibit the pursuit of scientific study? Are people too busy trying to survive to spend time on anything more than basic observations, or might someone in authority be preventing study through rule of law?

___

2. Do they know how the world around them works?

Do they know that there is more without having much of a glimpse yet, or do they know what atoms and molecules are? Are they able to see beyond what is visible with the naked eye?

___

The A-Zs of Worldbuilding

3. If there is no scientific knowledge, how are things explained?

What explanations are offered for disease, astronomical anomalies, or even fire?

_____

_____

_____

_____

_____

_____

_____

_____

_____

4. How technologically advanced is your world and/or society?

What stage of knowledge are they at? Do they know basic wound care, but not necessarily why they might get infected?

_____

_____

_____

_____

_____

_____

_____

_____

_____

5. Do they have ways to run experiments?

Is there protocol set up for reliably running tests, repeating them, and falsifying them?

6. Do they have a way to transfer information from one place to another, quicker than by physical means?

Are they using messenger pigeons or teleportation? Some types of experiments may be impossible with less-than-instantaneous communication across great distances.

The A-Zs of Worldbuilding

7. How does their science differ from ours?

For example: Do they have the same scientific laws? If not, are they correct or not?

8. Do they practice science the same way, or differently?

What steps are required? Observation, creating hypotheses, the creation of scientific theories and laws, etc. Some things may not be as important as in your world, depending on priorities and how scientific methods evolved.

9. Is science a discipline of study?

Or is it considered to be a hobby for the upper classes? Are scientists respected or ridiculed (like the alchemists of old)?

10. What branches of science are pursued?

An agrarian society will prioritize animal science and agricultural science, for example. A mining society would prioritize geology, etc.

The A-Zs of Worldbuilding

11. Do science *and* magic exist, or only one of them?

If they do both exist, do they work together at all, or are they completely separate entities?

12. If their science is actually magic, how does that affect their world?

Our world has DNA as the building blocks of life, how would that differ if the source were magical? Is magic something that can be tracked, manipulated, cloned?

13. What types of magic exist in your world?

Elemental magic is common for stories featuring nature. White/black magic (does this play into religious or moral issues at all?), blood magic, necromancy, etc.? Your options are pretty much endless, so use your imagination!

___

14. What is the source of magic?

Why does it exist? Is it something that people are innately born with, or is the source outside of them? Is it a constant source, or can the supply be interrupted? Can it be depleted?

___

The A-Zs of Worldbuilding

15. Who can use magic and why?

Is it an innate talent for everyone in your world, or is it limited to certain people or creatures? Can someone learn to use magic, or do they have to be predisposed to it?

_____
_____
_____
_____
_____
_____
_____
_____
_____

16. What is the cost of magic?

Magic will expend energy in some manner – whether it is someone's life force, or transferring energy from one place to another.

_____
_____
_____
_____
_____
_____
_____
_____
_____

17. What happens when magic misfires?

Can magic not do what it was expected to do? What types of consequences might happen? Has magic ever accidentally killed someone, or maybe turned them into a toad?

18. Is it possible to hinder or remove someone's ability to use magic?

How would this be accomplished? Would it be possible for anyone to perform this, or only for certain people? What might necessitate removing someone's magical ability? How might this type of power be abused?

The A-Zs of Worldbuilding

19. What social stigmas will arise with the presence of magic?

Are magic users rare, and therefore feared as something unknown? Or they might be revered! If everyone has some magic capability, but someone doesn't, are they ostracized?

___

20. What is the greatest good AND the greatest evil magic has ever caused?

Did it end a plague? Provide food for a starving society? Or perhaps it unleashed a plague or famine. How did it affect the history of your world, and the evolution of society?

___

21. What resources are you using for science and magic in your world?

T is for Time
Keeping Track of 'When'

Creating a sense of passing time is a necessary skill in fiction writing, but you don't want it to take too long for your reader to figure out what's happening.

With speculative fiction, and especially if you *like* worldbuilding, the urge is often there to change everything just because you can. But just because you can doesn't mean you should. Again: Don't change so much that your readers can't relate to your setting or your characters.

Seasons

The beginning and ending of seasons are usually determined by the solar solstices and equinoxes, unless you put a completely different solar system into place within your world. Weather can also act independently of the solstice or equinox if other circumstances are just right.

The closer you go to a pole (such as the North or South Pole), the shorter and milder summer weather will be, and the longer and colder the winters. The closer you are to an equator, the hotter it will be in general, even in the winter.

Now, if your world isn't round, or has some skewed sun revolutions, you're going to have to take that into account. But I am not an astronomer, so you're on your own there.

Marking the passing of seasons is not going to be as important in societies that are on an equatorial line, or places that are completely isolated from the elements (such as a spaceship), unless it is culturally important to them.

Tracking Time

Time can be measured in two ways – by machine (such as through the use of clocks), or by watching the changing signs in nature.

Our bodies are really designed to work in tune with nature, but we've ruined that with our electric lights and nine-to-five jobs. An agrarian society, though, would function almost exclusively in tune with nature, except when necessity demands they conform to the official timekeeping of society.

The natural passage of time may appear in different ways for different species and societies, and using whatever is the most prominent marker of time – whether that is sunrises and sunsets, how often a drop of water might fall from somewhere, or perhaps even a heartbeat. Mechanical timekeeping will develop from that – a method to track time the way are they are used to doing so, but without them having to keep a count going continuously.

Measuring time by nature doesn't mean just sunrise and sunset, and lunar cycles and watching the stars. It also means observing what is happening around them. Certain insects are only active during specific times of day, and some even during specific times of the year. Plants change and grow, especially with increasing temperatures. Knowing which wild plants are in season during which times of year will also help someone know the time – and when something might be abnormal.

Non-humanoid creatures may also instinctively track time. Wild animals don't have clocks, but they know when the seasons will change, and they begin preparing for it ahead of time. Don't underestimate the power of instinctual timekeeping, especially if your inhabitants are based on other creatures.

Calendars

Unless you're writing science fiction, or fantasy where they have space travel, you won't need to worry much about how the size of a planet and the speed of its rotation affects the length of a day. But it is something you can play around with if you *really* want, and if you're good at math.

The first thing you need to do is decide the length of day, and then how your culture splits that day up into measurable portions. The most obvious dividers are dawn, high noon, sunset, and midnight. If you have more than one moon or sun, it can give things an interesting twist, too.

Beyond that, you need to know the length of a year (how many seasons and/or months at the least, possibly how many days as well). Years are fairly universal in function – they make up the single rotation through a set of seasons, and it really doesn't matter which season begins or ends a year. Oftentimes, there are religious or seasonal reasons for when a year starts or ends. If you've already worked on some of your holidays and/or seasons, look at those and figure out why people would want to start or end on a certain one.

Culturally, people often gravitate toward starting a new year when something new is already on the horizon. Many cultures in our world start the new year with the arrival of the winter solstice, when the days begin to lengthen again. Or in spring, when the new crops are ready to be sown. There are some, though, who celebrate the beginning of a new year when something is finishing – perhaps after all the fall harvests are in and safely stored. Sometimes they even change the new year in commemoration of an event that changed their culture/world.

A word of advice: Leap years are really fun to play with, and can lend some interesting twists to your plot, but unless you've found a software that can accommodate assembling a timeline with leap years, and calculate which years a leap year would fall (since sci-fi/fantasy stories tend to have really long, rich histories and spans of time in play), you should proceed with caution. It can be a time-consuming process to figure out past and future dates when necessary. It's not impossible, though, so just know what you're getting into ahead of time.

The numbering of years is something to consider, but it's fairly simple – just decide how many years in a calendar system you want to have passed already. If you have a historically-heavy plot, look at the things you know already need to have happened and how many years beforehand so you can get an idea of the scope you need to allow for.

Once you know how your seasons are set up and when the year begins and ends, you can figure out how to break time down further – into months and weeks. Technically, the term 'week' is the designation for a seven-day period, but for this purpose it can be anything that you use to break a month down into more measurable time periods. The word month also comes from the word for 'moon' and basically means a moon-cycle.

Some cultures don't use weeks, though – they may only mark time by the phases of the moon (if your world has a moon, of course). This is one of those cases where you will need to decide if changing all the names of familiar things is worth it. Sometimes it can lend to the atmosphere of a story, but changing too many names can also cause confusion for your readers.

When it comes to naming your days and months (or anything else in your calendar that you wish to name), it's fairly simple. If you've toyed with your world's language(s), you can call everything after the names of deities or rulers, or just literally call them one, two, three, etc., in those languages. It's as complex or as simple as you'd like!

Time & Your Characters

In addition to how time is tracked, keep in mind how time flows from the perspective of your characters. Aging is directly related to time, and that perception of time is also going to affect how death is viewed.

If you give your inhabitants a shorter lifespan (say anywhere from 15-30 years), then while an early death may be sad, it may not be the tragic event that a species with a longer lifespan of perhaps 70-200 years. Make sure to keep how quickly your people mature in proportion with their lifespan.

As for immortal peoples (or those with a lifespan so long they practically are immortal), they will perceive time in an entirely different manner. In those cases, the passage of time will likely be accented more by the death of mortal things they love – whether it is a pet, or a lover.

Other Inspiration

There have been many fascinating ways thought up in the past for marking the passage of time. Sundials were popular for a long time before mechanical clocks came into common use. There have also been candles that have marks for each hour that it burns, but those are less reliable. Sometimes you can only mark the passage of time by how light or dark it is outside.

There are exceptions, in fiction, to some of these rules as well. Science fiction can do some really fun things with time, since time can be considered one of the dimensions in which we exist. George R.R. Martin uses seasons that span *years* of time as the basis for his popular series. And, well, if winter was coming and you knew it was going to last for *years* rather than weeks, it would certainly change your outlook on preparation and survival.

'Time' Exercises

1. How is the start of each season determined?

Is it determined by the solstice or equinox? The first rain, snow, or perhaps the first green sprouts of spring? Supernatural signs? The beginning or end of the harvest season?

_____
_____
_____
_____
_____
_____
_____
_____
_____

2. How long are the seasons?

The general rule of thumb is that seasons are close to the same length, with some slight variance depending on the local climate.

_____
_____
_____
_____
_____
_____
_____
_____

3. Would they, for any reason, have more than the standard four seasons?

Think: spring, summer, winter, autumn. Reasons for extra seasons might be supernatural (the curse of a deity) or an extra-long solar or lunar cycle. Don't forget to consider how it might will affect food production.

_____
_____
_____
_____
_____
_____
_____
_____
_____
_____

4. If the lengths of their seasons are inconsistent, does it affect the length of months or years at all?

Is a year determined by the number of days or months, or by the seasonal cycles?

_____
_____
_____
_____
_____
_____
_____
_____
_____
_____

5. What is their day length?

Is it shorter or longer than our 24 hours? How does it affect their physiology?

6. Do they divide their days up into measurable portions of time, or is it simply marked by the rising or setting of the sun or moon, and when each is at its highest point?

Think hours, minutes, and seconds, or dawn, high noon, sundown, and midnight. Use whatever equivalent you come up with that is appropriate for your world.

The A-Zs of Worldbuilding

7. How do they measure time?

There needs to be some way to mark the passage of time – whether by sundial, candles that burn a specified rate per hour (a drafty home would make this method unreliable, however), clocks, or calendars.

_____

_____

_____

_____

_____

_____

_____

_____

8. For your sanity, figure out a basic calendar with seasons marked so you can keep track of timing in your plot.

Basics recommended are days/weeks/months in an annual format, with the seasons. You can include lunar and solar cycle notations as well, if you wish.

_____

_____

_____

_____

_____

_____

_____

_____

9. What time and timekeeping resources are you using for your worldbuilding?

U is for Universe
Beyond the Horizon

'Universe' can have two meanings among fiction writers. It can mean the setting of a story or series with its specific rules (, and that is applicable to your worldbuilding because you must stay within the set of rules you've established. However, that's not the universe we'll be talking about in this chapter.

We're going to talk *universe* – literally.

If you're writing anything where there is interplanetary travel, you're going to have to put much more work into this section. If you're just writing a story that takes place on a single planet, and they use celestial bodies to track time, and seasons, and portents, then you don't need to worry about the next galaxy over.

Either way, though, you should still be aware of basic astronomical functions.

If you're writing hard science fiction, you're going to need to dig out some science books and talk to some experts. Your audience can be brutal, and it's important that you have your details and facts correct.

If you're writing fantasy, you have a bit more leeway, but once more, you must be consistent with the rules you have set into place for your world and story.

Your first step is to look at the story you've created and the setting for it, and then take a step back. Figure out what other aspects might come into play, even minutely, from other countries and continents. But don't spend too much time here, unless you know it's going to be important to your plot later.

Then take another step back. Now you should be 'seeing' your world as a whole – whether round, flat, or whatever you've decided. You should also be observing the celestial bodies that have a direct impact on your world – sun, moon, observable stars.

You can keep 'stepping back' as far as you need to for your story (or to satisfy your curiosity), but don't go so far that you actually lose sight of what your story is about.

Be aware of complications that may arise from having multiple suns, multiple moons, or sometimes even none of those at all. Life will be different from the way we think of it here on earth.

Multiple suns may mean very long, hot days, or multiple equators, or even one very hot equator. No moon would potentially mean no tides, or very different types of tides, depending on other gravitational pulls near the planet. Multiple moons might result in some very interesting tides, especially if the moons differ in size and create different gravitational pulls.

Other Inspiration

Read books. This is where reading science fiction will be good, even if you don't have the slightest inclination to write it, just to open up your mind to the possibilities you have by playing with different aspects of your universe. But, once again, don't get too bogged down on things that won't affect your story at all.

'Universe' Exercises

1. What is your world like, on a universe-scale?

If someone were to look at your world from outer space, what would they see? Does an 'outer space' even exist?

2. How does your world work?

What is the atmosphere like? How is the world shaped? What is the length of its rotations? Refer back to your Time exercises (pg. 195) because the rotations will affect the length of day.

The A-Zs of Worldbuilding

3. What is the universe like?
What are the nearby planets, if any? If someone were to look up at the sky from the surface of your world, what would they see?

_____
_____
_____
_____
_____
_____
_____
_____
_____
_____

4. What about a sun and moon, and/or other celestial bodies?
How do celestial bodies affect the weather of your world? How does it affect the daily lives of your characters?

_____
_____
_____
_____
_____
_____
_____
_____
_____
_____

5. What is daytime like? Nighttime?

How long is each one, and what are special considerations for dawn, noon, dusk, and midnight that might need to be in place, dependent on your universe?

___

6. How much of the universe have your characters explored?

Not even necessarily the characters you're using in your story, but the people you've populated your world with. It's fine if they've never left the surface of their planet.

___

The A-Zs of Worldbuilding

7. If they are still earthbound, what types of speculation exist about the universe?
What do they think might be 'out there?'

8. Is there something 'out there' whether your characters know it or not?
Aliens? God? Anything, nothing?

9. What are your resources for building your universe?

V is for Visual Arts
Creating & Preserving Beauty

Living is fine, but beauty is what captivates us. There's a reason dystopian fiction has very little beauty in its settings – because the author is trying to portray hopelessness and discouragement. There may be moments of beauty, but they often serve to make the hopelessness starker.

Extreme beauty can also be used to convey heartbreak or utter despair.

Visual arts (any type of art your characters observe with their eyes) within a story's setting are vital; they will convey the tone and feel of your world as much by their absence as they will by their presence.

Arts as Enjoyment

Never underestimate the power of art to help people feel content. It can transport them to another place and another time, and often that place is happier than the moment they are living.

Some art is simply present because someone thinks it is beautiful – no deeper meaning required. I have a picture hanging in my dining room that came with the house when my husband and I bought it, and I was actually thrilled it was still there after we signed all the papers and received the keys. I'd seen it hanging on the wall the first time we viewed the house, and instantly loved the picture.

Arts as Commemoration

Common symbols and icons used will often have some origin in religion, myth, or superstition. The use of certain symbols usually follows certain eras and trends, and possibly certain religions. Every person who has had some exposure to Catholicism knows a picture is a Madonna when they see a seated woman holding a baby with a raised hand.

Monuments and sculptures are often raised at the sites of great battles, remembering either the conqueror or the lives lost, or sometimes both. It all depends on which side erected it.

A famous person – whether religious, political, mythical, beautiful, or rich – will inspire art. The more tragic their story, often the more 'inspiring' people find them to be.

Art is also used to immortalize something that is greatly loved. It can be transformed into something that will last long after the finite is gone. Though not even art lasts forever.

Arts as Propaganda

Everyone knows the swastika – though it can mean completely different things depending on the culture. Many people are familiar with mandalas, as well.

Each of those are icons and symbols used by cultures for specific purposes, but they are often incorporated into artwork. The dominant religion in a culture will also have a great effect on public arts – think of the Sistine Chapel and Michelangelo's other works, especially. Much of his artwork was based on religious themes.

Art is also used to confront fear. It is often given much power by the superstitious. Gargoyles lined the eaves of cathedrals in days past to guard against demons. Sometimes realistic paintings are considered to be apparitions of the dead. Maybe something made with certain materials can become a portal, or a prison.

Art as Culture

Many times, a distinctive type of art will develop within a culture or society. One of the ways archeologist can identify a people group is by how they decorated, especially with the embellishments added to garments, pottery, weapons, etc.

The method the art is created will depend on the natural resources of the area where your inhabitants have settled, and then it will depend on their level of technology. Images and designs will stay essentially the same, but will become more easily produced.

Cultural art will be dependent on cultural values. Those values may be influenced by religion but they don't have to be. The use of idols in worship, particularly at personal altars or shrines, or even the forbidden use of such images can create a culture where images are divine (and therefore either mimicked everywhere, or are limited in use to only divine beings) or where images – even portraits – are not present in art forms.

Some cultures may become more focused on different themes or forms, like nature, calligraphy, or mosaics. A coastal culture might mimic the sea in much of their artwork.

Other Inspiration

Take an afternoon and indulge in some of your favorite visual art – whether watching a favorite movie, reading a favorite book, or visiting a museum that has a collection you greatly enjoy. Make notes of things that really leap out to you – figure out what your favorite elements are and how they make you feel.

Then take some time and look at some art you *don't* enjoy. Not necessarily things that are *bad* (and absolutely don't look at anything that might be a trigger for you!) but things that just don't make you feel the same things that your favorite art does. Figure out why you don't like them.

Now take both of those elements, and use them to develop the art that your culture(s) creates.

'Visual Arts' Exercises

1. What is the lifestyle of your inhabitants?

Nomadic peoples are not going to haul around large paintings with them – they're more likely to put their art on functional items. It will be woven into the panels of their tents, or painted on the sides of their pots. They may have very vivid, colorful clothing with intricate embroidery. If someone is creating art in an established city, then they might be creating murals and portraits for patrons.

2. What materials do they have access to for creating art?

Art can be made with anything, though more permanent forms of art will require certain parameters. A picture can be easily scratched in the dirt, but it's not going to last unless it's a fired clay tablet, for example. Cloth can be a medium as well – woven or embroidered tapestries, blankets, tents, etc. Some of this will depend on the level of technology your culture has developed.

3. What do your people love?

Certain things will often be revered by an entire people group. This is what will help generate a popular form of art.

_____
_____
_____
_____
_____
_____
_____
_____
_____
_____

4. What do your people fear?

The thing a religion promises deliverance for will be one of the things people fear most. Mythology will also be a good place to start, as well as anything unexplained that has killed people, whether that unexplained thing is a disease, or a creature.

_____
_____
_____
_____
_____
_____
_____
_____
_____

The A-Zs of Worldbuilding

5. What kind of art do they simply like, without any deeper meaning or agenda?

It can still be something representative of their culture, though. Perhaps a national flower, or bird, that frequently shows up in artwork because they enjoy its appearance.

6. Is there anything that is considered 'taboo' for artwork?

Certain types of work might be censored for public decency, or even considered blasphemous. What if artwork itself is not allowed? Is there a black market for it? How would it have evolved?

7. What resources are you using to develop visual art in your world?

W is for Weapons & Warfare
Arming Your Characters for the Story

Weapons and warfare are a part of any society. As long as flawed creatures inhabit your world, weapons will be created and used against one another in some way.

Weapons will exist outside of war, though. They are also used to butcher livestock and to hunt, even to cook. Some are used to harvest plants – a scythe is pretty scary looking, but its original purpose was to cut stalks of wheat, not reap the souls of the dead.

Pretty much anything can become a weapon in the hands of a determined individual, though. Even if its original purpose was something else, and even if it isn't a *convenient* weapon.

The Need for Weapons

Different societies and cultures will need different things. Once again, what is made will depend on what is available for materials.

What is needed and why? Unless a society is completely vegetarian (unlikely, but possible) there will need to be a way to kill animals for meat. Ethical groups will make this as quick and painless for an animal as possible, and that means sharp blades.

Slaughtered animals will also then need to be cleaned and skinned (or feathers or fur/hair removed from the skin). Skinning is definitely the quickest way to prepare a carcass for eating, but it also requires a sharp knife.

Weapons for warfare tend to be more brutal. People are harder to kill than animals (except maybe lions and bears). They survive more, and a wounded enemy is more dangerous than a dead one. No one uses a double-edged sword as their first choice to slaughter an animal. That is a weapon created specifically for war.

Keep in mind that weapons do not have to be something that is held in someone's hands, either. Magic can be a formidable force when wielded in the proper form, and there is also the matter of weapons of mass destruction. It doesn't have to be a bomb – it can be a poison or pathogen dumped in the main water supply.

Crafting Weapons

Without a consistent, obtainable source of metal, weapons will be more 'primitive.' There will be clubs, quarterstaffs, bows and arrows, and slingshots. All of these things can be functional without actual metal incorporated. An arrowhead can be as simple as a sharpened end of wood, or a piece of flint bound to the arrow shaft. Don't underestimate the power of a simple slingshot, though. All that is required for this is some sort of string or cord, a piece of leather, and ammunition (which is usually rocks). If someone is accurate with a slingshot, it can be lethal.

Metal weapons are the most valuable, and the most difficult to make. It requires someone who knows smithery, unless you have a magical workaround in your world.

Smithery requires a way to put together a forge, and that's not something easily transportable. A blacksmith is a huge asset to a community, though – they don't make *just* weapons. They will make nails, tools, even cookware. As a side note, historically smiths would also work as farriers. Farriers would create and apply horseshoes and provide some veterinary care as well.

Warfare

Fighting styles develop according to the landscape where a culture exists. Long, open distances make it necessary for a cavalry to exist, preferably with long-range weapons. Terrain with hills or trees means people need to be able to fight well on foot. If a group lives in a forest, though, they will have a huge advantage if they can fight from the trees.

Most of all, they will know how to use their native landscape to their advantage. High altitudes will potentially compromise attackers who are from lower altitudes, since they won't be able to quickly adjust to the lack of oxygen in the air.

Heat and cold each have their respective pros and cons. Once again, it's all about acclimation. Deprive an opposing force of water in the heat? Half the battle is already won with very little actual physical conflict. Prevent a force from finding shelter in extreme cold? You probably won't even have to fight at all.

Who Is Taught?

Who is allowed to learn the use of weapons can be a plot point. If women aren't allowed to learn, then a woman coming in (or learning on the sly) can be quite a shock. Perhaps a society is matriarchal, instead, and men have limitations on what they can and can't do. Eligibility may also be determined by birth – social rank can play a large role in who is permitted or forbidden to learn, but a society may also see battle prowess as something that is passed through a blood line or genetics.

There can also be age restrictions, ability restrictions (long-term battling is not a simple physical feat – it requires extensive training to build up stamina), or perhaps who learns what is determined by simply drawing a name from a hat. Systems will develop, depending on the governing authorities and what is most advantageous for them. Even if an armed force was originally created with the intention of protecting the common people, at some point those in power will do their best to wrest control of it for themselves.

Other Inspiration

Research the types of weapons used by any cultures you've drawn inspiration from so far, and from cultures with similar landscape, resources, and climates. Bows would be a huge 'no' in a climate where it's constantly raining, and keeping metal weapons from rusting would also be a feat.

Be creative with forms of weapons, but keep in mind that some things will have extra complications. Swords that look like giant serrated knives would actually be very difficult to use because they'd be very *hard* to pull out of someone's body.

'Weapons & Warfare' Exercises

1. What resources are available for making weapons?

If there are no trees, there will be no bows. If there is no metal, there will be no swords. Simple knives and clubs can be made from stone.

_____
_____
_____
_____
_____
_____
_____
_____

2. What are the three most common weapons?

Keep these factors in mind: whether or not weapons are easily available to everyday people, how much they cost to acquire, and how easily they can be made.

_____
_____
_____
_____
_____
_____
_____
_____

W is for Weapons & Warfare

3. What one weapon is your culture/people group *really good* at making, whether they are well-known for it or not?

This will probably have started off as something functional – maybe they make really good axes because they had to cut down a lot of very sturdy trees. Or they make really great bows and arrows because it was too dangerous to get close to their main source of food.

___
___
___
___
___
___
___
___
___

4. If you're only focusing on worldbuilding for one culture for your story, who makes the best swords? The best bows? The truest arrows? Why?

Who would your people go to outside of themselves to source good weapons that they can't make?

___
___
___
___
___
___
___
___
___

5. How does the local terrain affect the fighting style?

What advantages and disadvantages would the terrain pose in a battle? Refer to the Geography exercises (pg. 57) as necessary.

_____
_____
_____
_____
_____
_____
_____
_____
_____

6. When have they been forced to adapt their fighting style?

Did someone attack who was better prepared for their terrain than expected? What if they were forced out of their own lands, and had to fight somewhere completely new?

_____
_____
_____
_____
_____
_____
_____
_____
_____

7. Who is allowed (or not allowed) to learn to fight? Why or why not?

What is the cultural basis for those rules? Is it correct, or incorrect, and how can you use it to benefit your story, or hinder your characters? (Not all hindrances are bad! Consider it a challenge to be overcome.)

_____

_____

_____

_____

_____

_____

_____

_____

_____

_____

8. What level of knowledge or experience is required before one is considered to be a 'warrior'?

How long must someone train or serve before they are considered fully-fledged? Is it something that takes years (like a form of martial art), or something that can be learned in a matter of months?

_____

_____

_____

_____

_____

_____

_____

_____

9. Utilize the blank space below to sketch out some ideas of how your weapons might look. *Even if you can't draw well, just put down some basic shapes and descriptions.*

10. What resources are you using from our world for your weapons and warfare?

X is for Xenial
Concerning the Hospitality of Guests

The word 'xenial' has to do with hospitality. Specifically, it can pertain to the type of hospitality shown to strangers and guests. Since travel is an integral part of many speculative fiction plots, hospitality is an important thing to consider in your worldbuilding. We will look at both day-to-day hospitality and hospitality shown to guests and travelers.

Common Courtesy

There are many different ways people say hello or goodbye, as well as potential cultural reasons why they don't say either of those things. It can be complicated or simple, and perhaps it ties in with other cultural occurrences. There may also be additional greetings included, such as during a holiday season (Merry Christmas!)

Depending on how your society is set up, there may be common *mandatory* courtesies for those of different rank. Think of whether royalty must be addressed in a certain manner, and if people are required to bow or curtsy. If someone is seen as having descended directly from a divine being, perhaps culture demands that people fully prostrate themselves in their presence.

There may be those who are not acknowledged publicly at all – like servants, peasants, or beggars. There are multitudes of reasons a society might see certain people as inferior, sadly.

Attitudes and language in general can be more or less formal, and may depend on how well people know each other, the capacity they are interacting in at that moment, societal rank, or gender.

When devising protocol and courtesies between ranking individuals and their equals or subjects, keep in mind that many things will be shaped to lessen the *fear* of the risk of assassination. Words and phrases that are perfectly acceptable in common company may be perceived as threatening when in the presence of ranking individuals.

Treatment of Guests

A guest can be a familiar friend, in which case they will not require much formality, but there still may be certain things that are offered because of custom. Casual greetings can be a simple 'hi' or even greeting someone by name. But universal hospitality may be inviting someone to sit down and asking if they'd like a drink, regardless of whether they are a close friend or a new acquaintance.

Travelers, especially strangers, will receive a different kind of hospitality, and that can vary. If a town has been repeatedly pillaged or taken advantage of, they won't be very friendly to strangers anymore. But some places might pride themselves on their hospitality, and will go all out to impress a guest.

In an agrarian society, or any place that uses livestock as their main form of transportation, it would be more than reasonable for a stranger to be offered feed, water, and a place in the stable for their animal. A drink, meal, and perhaps even a bath (or foot washing) are things that would be offered to nearly everyone, no matter what their rank.

However, if a monarch were to suddenly show up at the front door, it may even be an occasion to slaughter an animal for dinner, even if it was being saved for some other occasion. Not every guest is going to receive *that* kind of hospitality.

A family member who just showed up out of the blue, though, may not warrant very much special hospitality. It just depends. Hospitality and common courtesies are elements that can enhance a plot and the interactions between characters, as many different nuances and intentions can be made clear between what is offered, and what is not.

Another matter to consider is if and when guests can be turned away. It might be that certain guests may never be turned away – such as a monarch, though it would courteous of a gracious monarch to find lodging or sustenance elsewhere if there has been a death in the home recently.

Sickness will almost always be a reason to turn away guests. An illness potentially being contagious is nothing to ever mess around with, especially if medical care is not incredibly advanced.

The main thing to consider is whether one can turn away a guest for any reason, without *giving* a reason, or if they must have a concrete reason to do so.

Other Inspiration

Look up etiquette of different historical eras and different cultures – there's some unique customs out there that can be great story inspiration. Etiquette will also vary by social and economic status. There are certain customs some might find difficult to part with, even if they have experienced a change in social status. There is also the fact that the rich can afford more niceties.

The A-Zs of Worldbuilding

'Xenial' Exercises

1. Is there a ritual greeting and/or farewell?

How do people introduce themselves to each other, or part ways? In addition to spoken greetings, there may also be physical actions – bow/curtsy, handshakes, kisses, etc. Refer to the Language exercises (pg. 98) as necessary.

2. What determines status for hospitality reasons?

While those of high societal or noble rank may be of higher status, cultural hospitality may demand that even they defer to specific individuals. These individuals may be people like respected elders (especially where age is considered to be an indicator of wisdom), a respected religious leader, or a village wise woman (herbalist/witch). The infirm may also be given special accommodations.

3. What are the protocols for greeting someone of higher social rank?
This may vary dependent on how highly ranked an individual is.

4. What peoples/classes are considered inferior? Are they not greeted, or greeted privately in some circumstances?
This could be for nearly any reason – the poor, the infirm, women, children, etc.

The A-Zs of Worldbuilding

5. How can a guest initiate a stay with someone?

Perhaps it's frowned upon to just randomly ask to stay with someone, and certain steps must be taken first – like a proper introduction, or offering a gift to the host/hostess.

6. What amenities are customarily offered to guests?

A drink? Hot meal? A private bed or bath? A place to lodge their animals? How do those offerings vary by the class/social status of the guest?

7. When is it permissible to turn away guests?

A house in mourning, suffering illness, or without the supplies to properly care for a guest could all be reasons. Get creative!

8. What is the worst *faux pas* possible?

What would never be allowed, either in interacting with someone on the street, lodging a guest, or interacting with someone of rank?

The A-Zs of Worldbuilding

9. What has a cultural misunderstanding of hospitality created a political misunderstanding in your world?

Perhaps someone was greeted with a gesture that is common in one culture, but lewd in another, or someone was greeted too casually, or inappropriately for their gender.

10. How does gender (and possibly sexuality) affect acceptable hospitality?

One gender may be shown deference (offered a seat by the other gender, especially when there are none available, opening doors, etc.) or demeaned (not allowed to speak in the presence of another gender, etc.).

11. What resources are you using for creating hospitality customs?

Y is for Youth
Preparing the Next Generation

The establishment of future generations is the foundation of every society. Without children, there is no future, but those children grow up to be adults who take over the running of... everything.

In historical times, there has been a strong emphasis on raising children to be adults. In many cultures, there is no 'teenager' phase – one is simply a child until they are an adult. We've lost a lot of that somewhere in the last hundred years, at least in many first world countries where technology is rampant and convenience is nearly worshipped. Knowledge can be lost as quickly as it is gained when skills aren't passed on.

Despite that, we're still all familiar with the somewhat mystical concept of 'coming of age' when one realizes they are finally passing from childhood to adulthood.

Childhood

Some cultures may treat children as, essentially, small adults. But even in times when life is difficult, there seems to be consideration for allowing children to play. That said, it is easy to turn anything into a game, and some of the best childhood games are the ones where children are taught life skills in a fun way[13].

Eventually, children will hit a point where they aren't really children anymore, but they're not quite adults either. In American society especially, the teen years are considered this in-between stage. Some cultures will skip over this entirely, especially when there is an emphasis on survival rather than finding a purpose for life (such as a calling or specific career).

However, even when society doesn't have any allowances for this stage, it is still normal for someone to feel lost as they enter adulthood.

Coming of Age

The more technological a society becomes, the more the age of majority seems to be delayed (with some exceptions). The age of majority in the United States used to be 21, though it is now 18. However, in many third-world countries and cultures which prioritize procreation, one is considered to be an adult at the onset of puberty for boys, or the start of a girl's menses.

It can also be determined by whether they have completed a certain amount of schooling (8th grade, or graduating high school, perhaps even a sort of finishing school, depending on your culture), or by demonstrating certain skills (Can they build a home? Butcher an animal? Make sturdy clothing?)

There may also be rituals involved – perhaps completing a solo hunt, or a vision quest.

---

[13] Refer back to *O is for Oblectation*, pg. 128

Cultural Lifestyle

Culture affects how everything is viewed through the eyes of your characters. It shapes how children are raised, what expectations are for adulthood, and societal duties. Societies will embrace different types of milestones dependent on their cultural values.

A technologically advanced society will most likely value an accrual of knowledge, scientific discoveries, and technological inventions over anything else. The extensive use of technology seems to lead to a certain amount of disconnect from other accomplishments – such as maintaining a source of food.

An agrarian society will value the knowledge of how to produce food (including raising livestock for meat) and making sturdy shelters, as well as virility, over 'book knowledge.' Inhabitants may not embrace the ability to read or write until *not* being able to do so becomes a liability to their way of life. Until then, it may be seen as something that wastes time.

A warrior society will be adept at hunting, and they will value the ability to perform certain physical feats. Strength, brute force, and dexterity will be preferred traits. Warriors will find their value in battle, and boy may not become a man until he has seen bloodshed.

Additionally, in some cultures receiving a name is a rite of passage, and people may change their names at different points in their lives. It might be very unusual for a character to still go by the name they were given at birth once they have come of age, for example.

Rituals

In cultures that do have coming-of-age rituals, they are focused on the discovery of a purpose in their lives, or proving that they can provide for themselves and/or a potential family. Coming-of-age can be as simple as turning a certain age, but there is something about rituals that can be compelling and binding.

The act of a ritual serves the purpose of imprinting an event or a vow into a person. The memory of it will carry a significance that binds a person to a community and way of life, and is a way of preserving a culture and its values. It can be as simple as partaking in a celebration, or as serious as a blood oath.

If someone cannot complete a ritual, no matter whether their reason was legitimate or not, they may have to bear a heavy burden within their culture. Someone without the physical stamina to complete a hunting ritual may be seen as a liability in the community, particularly if they are disabled. Some may refuse to the coming of age ceremony, for whatever reason, and that in itself might be seen as rejecting the culture. In some cases, there may also be severe consequences – up to and including banishment or death.

Look into history as well – many Native American and African cultures valued vision quests as an initiation into adulthood. Vision quests are when a person seeks the guidance of a vision, or of spirits, for a decision.

The quest usually involves a physically challenge (a fast or withstanding extreme exposure to the elements, for example) and the ingestion of some sort of drug. The drug is used to open a person's senses to more experiences, and this is why psychotropic drugs are often the type chosen. Depending on the technological level of the society, the dosage of the drug may be unknown and it may also have unpredictable side effects.

Other Inspiration

Talk to family members – find out what was a defining moment in their own coming-of-age. It's easy to be unaware of your own cultural heritage until you ask about it. Even if there isn't a cultural heritage there, you may be surprised by the types of events that a coming-of-age seems to center around. It can be as simple as someone being told they are now an adult and being treated as such, or as complex as being thrown into adulthood because a tragedy forced them to mature quickly.

Sometimes, adulthood is seen as a loss of freedom as well – especially for women. Cultural expectations can sometimes be that a woman is to be a mother and little else, and so adulthood becomes very different from childhood when they are married off. It all depends on the cultural values you've established for the different societies in your world. Coming of age doesn't have to be difficult for your characters, but do be consistent with the cultural aspects you've already put into place.

'Youth' Exercises

1. What would the typical childhood look like in your culture?

What societal expectations are placed even on the very young? What types of activities would they have been allowed to participate in?

2. What age is considered to be on the cusp of adulthood?

This will be earlier in societies that place an emphasis on procreation (usually coinciding with puberty), and later in ones that value technological advances.

The A-Zs of Worldbuilding

3. Is there any specific criteria that must be met to be considered an adult? Does this differ by gender?

Any schooling, or proving proficiency with any particular set of skills, or even the onset of puberty, or the start of menses? Perhaps one gender is required to complete a hunt, all the way from tracking and killing, to butchering and preparing a meal from the prey. Another may be required to prove they can keep a home, including food preservation, and making clothing. Perhaps all genders must prove they can defend their homes and the people they love.

4. What rituals have developed around those criteria?

There are many of these rituals still in place in the modern world – birthday celebrations, especially for someone's 18th or 21st birthday, graduating from school, just to name a few.

5. How are these criteria embraced or challenged by the youth?

Is there a strong sense of cultural pride that is imbued into the youth? What might challenge that pride, and make them question the cultural criteria for adulthood? What might make them revere it?

6. Does the criteria make sense for the type of culture that is in place? If not, why?

A more technologically advanced society will value knowledge over physical feats. An agrarian society, though, will value muscle and hard labor, because it is necessary for survival. However, the age of a society may mean that something that was once culturally significant may now be just a forgotten ritual.

The A-Zs of Worldbuilding

7. What resources are you referring to for coming of age within your world?

Y is for Youth

Z is for Zoology
Enriching Your World with Animals

Personally, I find creating animals is one of the things I most enjoy about worldbuilding. Animals serve many purposes. They are a vital part of ecosystems, a source of food (whether directly, for meat, or indirectly, for milk), can be a source of clothing (leather, wool), and a source of companionship (pets). Animals are also used for protection of both family and livestock. Domesticated predators (such as dogs) are not the only options – donkeys and llamas are common livestock guardians as well.

As you worldbuild your animals, don't forget that nature has a tendency to balance things out. An abundance of prey will mean an abundance of predators. It's easy for ecosystems to become compromised, too, if a creature is introduced into a climate where it doesn't have a natural predator (say someone releases a few rodent pets into the wild on their travels). A system can be quickly overrun, and that may require a new predator – or new hunting practices – to be introduced as well.

Climates

The kind of animals present will depend on the climate, terrain, and resources. Where there is water, there will be fish. In warmer climates, there will be amphibians near the water (though you can create an amphibian that thrives in cooler temperatures if you like.) Cooler climates will mean animals with fur, a large body mass, and a thick layer of insulating fat to help generate and preserve heat.

Plains

Plains and prairies have the ability to support herd creatures that require extensive grazing grounds and extensive *space*. There may be fewer birds (but not *no* birds – there will be a lot of birds that don't rely as much on flight), plenty of rodents, and predators that can hide in tall grasses and burrows. There will be a lot of snakes. Canine type predators will be abundant in the plains, as well as crossing over into forest regions.

Forests

Trees mean birds – and lots of them. Birds like to perch on branches, they build nests in/on/out of trees, and they like to eat fruit from trees.

There will still be herd animals in forests – but think slender ones, like deer, rather than buffalo. Trees sometimes grow very closely together in the forest, and that makes it difficult for large creatures to get through. Big cats are more likely to be found in forest regions as well – African lions are really the anomaly in this sense. Forested regions have cougars, and tigers, and bobcats, just to name a few.

There may be snakes, depending on how cold winters get in the climate you've set up. There will be lots of rodents, both ground rodents (mice, rats) and climbing rodents (squirrels).

Tropics

Tropics are incredibly diverse! They are extremely fertile regions, which means there is both an abundance of food for herbivores/omnivores, and an abundance of prey for carnivores. The tropics are where you will find greater varieties of species that might also exist worldwide. Birds, primates, amphibians, reptiles – anything that can thrive in warm weather and high humidity year-round. There will still be grazing animals, as well.

Insects

Nearly all climates will have insects – even the very cold ones. Insects may only be a seasonal nuisance in the coldest climates, but they will still be present. They are incredibly resilient creatures, despite living for a relatively short amount of time. Their eggs can remain dormant for quite a while, only beginning development when the conditions are right (flea eggs are triggered by the presence of warm-blooded creatures, for example).

Insects are necessary pollinators, predators and pests, and prey. Many birds and small mammals thrive on insects as one of their main sources of food. Insects reproduce incredibly quickly, and in great numbers, which makes them an ideal source of food.

Insects can have a great impact on a story and on characters. What happens if an entire crop is swarmed and eaten? Inhabitants may starve, unless they can recover quickly enough. Blood-sucking insects can make someone downright miserable, and even cause anemia if someone is bitten enough.

Appearance

Where an animal lives will determine a lot about how they look – whether they have fur, skin, scales, hair, or feathers. Some of that will also depend on *how* an animal lives.

Water creatures will have scales or skin, or very oily feathers or fur to help keep them warm and dry. Herd creatures will usually have hooves, because their feet need extra protection because of how much walking they do.

Take the climate into consideration, and the types of elements and seasons a creature will be subjected to. Creatures that hibernate through a season will need the ability to store reserves that can maintain them while they sleep. Creatures that hunt will need a way to quickly incapacitate their prey (sharp teeth or claws, venom, etc.)

Don't Reinvent the Horse

One of the best ways to create creatures for your world is to take something you love from *this* world and then adjust it to fit your setting and your climate. Give it one major change so it's not the same creature as we have, and then make little tweaks.

It's also easy to fall into the trap of making creatures that are basically identical to what we are familiar with and then simply renaming them. That only makes it harder for your readers.

If it's a horse, call it a horse. There doesn't need to be a ridiculously hard name for it that makes it necessary to describe every minute detail until your reader wonders, "But isn't that a horse?"

Other Inspiration

Animals are fascinating, but don't get so enthusiastic that it clutters your story with insignificant details and hampers your reader's ability to comprehend – just like with any other aspect of worldbuilding.

Start with animals (or types of creatures) that are familiar, and that your characters will actually encounter in the story, whether they are animals for companionship or sustenance, domesticated or not.

The A-Zs of Worldbuilding

'Zoology' Exercises

1. What is the main climate your creatures and inhabitants will be dealing with?

Where is your story set? What types of seasonal changes will be present? How quickly do weather changes happen? You should have decided much of this in the Geography (pg. 54), Plants (pg. 138), and Time (pg. 192) chapters.

_____
_____
_____
_____
_____
_____
_____
_____
_____
_____

2. What types of predators are present?

Are there a lot of wild cats? Giant lizards (dinosaurs!), or blood-sucking things? Birds of prey?

_____
_____
_____
_____
_____
_____
_____
_____
_____

3. What do the predators hunt?

This will often be herd animals, or a pest creature that is present in abundance.

4. What types of creatures are typically raised for meat?

This can be anything – rabbit-type creatures, herd animals, birds, fish... It will depend mostly on the resources available to feed and maintain them.

The A-Zs of Worldbuilding

5. What is the most unique-looking creature?
Not ugly, but definitely not something that is commonplace. Like a duck-billed platypus.

6. What is the most exotic creature your main character(s) has ever seen?
Whether it pertains to the story or not.

7. What creature is *everywhere*?
Think sparrows. And mice. Ants.

8. What creature is so rarely seen most people don't think it actually exists?
One word: dragons. Anything that might have magical properties, especially if magic has fallen away from use in your fictional world.

The A-Zs of Worldbuilding

9. What zoology resources are you using for your worldbuilding?

Congratulations!

You made it to the end!

If you've completed all 26 exercises, you have a world to write in that is fleshed out and ready for your story. Even if you haven't finished all of the sets, but only used the portions that felt natural for your story, you're well prepared.

Worldbuilding doesn't have to end here – this is really just scratching the surface. We barely delved into magic, for one. Keep asking yourself 'what if' and writing down the answers and ideas you come up with.

If you've discovered a new, addicting hobby through this workbook – I'm sorry. (Not really.) Have fun, and don't forget to go back to actually writing your story!

You can download additional copies of the worldbuilding exercises on my blog[14].

If you'd like to connect with other worldbuilders and get interactive feedback, please do check out the Worldbuilding Wednesday[15] events on my blog.

If this book was helpful to you, I'd really appreciate it if you left a review at any of these places: Amazon.com, Barnes & Noble, Goodreads, and/or any of your favorite book review sites!

Thank you so much!

Rebekah Loper

---

[14] rebekahloper.com/a-z-worldbuilding-downloads (password: 2017worldbuilding)
[15] rebekahloper.com/worldbuilding-wednesdays

About the Author

Rebekah Loper began creating fictional worlds and magical stories as a child and she never stopped. Now she also helps inspire others to write their stories through her volunteer work as a NaNoWriMo Municipal Liaison.

Rebekah lives in Tulsa, Oklahoma with her husband, a dog, a formerly feral cat, a flock of chickens, and an extensive tea collection. She can often be found cursing the existence of Bermuda grass as she battles the elements to create a productive, permaculture urban farm on a shoestring budget.

She blogs about writing and urban farming/homesteading at rebekahloper.com, and is a contributing blogger at Fantasy-Faction.com and the Rabid Rainbow Ferret Society (fictionalferrets.wordpress.com).

Follow her on Facebook (facebook.com/RebekahLoper), Instagram (rebekah.loper), and Twitter (rebekah_loper).

Made in the USA
Columbia, SC
30 May 2020